THE IMAGE OF ARIZONA

THE
IMAGE
OF
ARIZONA

Pictures from the Past

by
ANDREW WALLACE

Albuquerque

UNIVERSITY OF NEW MEXICO PRESS

Endpapers: Front—"Cavalry in an Arizona Sandstorm," wood engraving after Frederic Remington (*Harper's Weekly,* September 14, 1889). Back—"Sierra Bonita Ranch," lithograph by an unknown artist (Elliott's *History of Arizona Territory,* 1884).

ACKNOWLEDGMENTS

The immediate source of each picture is indicated in its accompanying caption, but I wish to acknowledge some extraordinary assistance in procuring many of the illustrations.

The libraries of Northern Arizona University and the Museum of Northern Arizona at Flagstaff provided most of the pictures for this volume, and I wish to thank especially Mr. Ezra Fitch, in charge of reference services and interlibrary loans at the university, for his constant aid. At the museum, Miss Katherine Bartlett's assistance was invaluable.

Several rare publications were found in the library of the Arizona Pioneers' Historical Society at Tucson, and I must thank Mr. Charles C. Colley, archivist of the collection, for help in locating and copying important pictures. Mr. Joseph F. Park, curator of the Western collection in the library of the University of Arizona, was helpful in copying pictures from *Outing* magazine.

Also in Tucson I was fortunate in the assistance of Mr. William A. Duffen and Mr. James E. Serven, private collectors whose libraries yielded unique treasures.

For the privilege of copying the title page of the first book published in Arizona, I am indebted to the Pimeria Alta Historical Society of Nogales and to its president, Mr. Charles S. Wise.

Mrs. Marguerite B. Cooley, Arizona State Librarian, unearthed the original architectural drawing for the capitol in her vault and made it available to me.

Finally I wish to thank Mr. Gary Topping who, while a graduate student at Northern Arizona University, helped locate many of the picture sources.

Andrew Wallace

CONTENTS

THE IMAGE OF ARIZONA

INTRODUCTION

NO ONE IS NEUTRAL in his feeling about Arizona, this land of desert and mountain. Everyone is affected positively by the solitude of canyons or by shimmering sunswept vistas. An Appalachian wilderness may exude quiet beauty, or a Midwestern landscape may arrange itself in natural loveliness, but they are scenes one can accept or ignore. In Arizona the atmosphere itself assaults the skin and sinuses, the mineral colors in sunlight dazzle the eyes, and the full moon draws wraiths from adobe ruins.

Today the editors of *Arizona Highways* magazine abandon written description and present the natural wonders in photographic opulence. But how did the pre-camera graphic reporters of the nineteenth century transmit their impressions?

It was through prints—from woodblocks, copperplates, and stone lithographs—that Americans everywhere first became acquainted with the Southwest. Well into the twentieth century many Americans still saw Arizona only through a limited number of oft-repeated pictures. The earliest photographs have been printed only recently in books and magazines, changing and expanding the image of the past.

No photograph taken in Arizona has been assigned a date earlier than 1861; apparently few were made before 1870. And it still surprises many historians that wood engraving as a medium of illustration reached its pinnacle in the two decades after 1880. Thus it was from woodcuts that the majority of people learned how Arizona and its inhabitants looked.

This volume makes no pretense of being a comprehensive written text on the history of territorial Arizona, nor is it a scholarly study of the artists themselves who depicted Arizona before 1912. Readers familiar with the companion volumes of the University of New Mexico Press on the early pictorial history of New Mexico and Colorado will recognize that this book is devoted to the published illustrations contemporary with Southwestern history since about 1831. When, in the latter year, Timothy Flint edited and published *The Personal Narrative of James O. Pattie of Kentucky* . . . and embellished it with five wood engravings of dubious accuracy, he kindled a curiosity not soon to be satisfied by more accurate reports or photographs.

I have endeavored to cull from the literature, the press, and government documents of seventy-five years the non-photographic pictures that best represented Arizona at the time. Fortune smiled on some scenes and preserved eyewitness views that are indeed primary documents for historical study.

Being chiefly black and white, and usually in line, the pictures in this book may provide future authors and publishers with a source of significant and easily reproduced illustrations that are in the public domain. Perhaps my commentary on and identification of the sources of the pictures will make them as useful to serious students of Arizona history as are the more common photographs.

I. THE NATIVE DWELLERS

"An Apache Indian" by Frederic Remington (*Harper's Monthly,* 1891).

"Los Apaches" was the Spanish name for the Southwest's most dangerous inhabitants, and "human tigers" was how the Anglo-Americans characterized these Indians. Unfortunately an ugly blood stain traverses every phase of Arizona's early Indian history. The Apache, however, were not the most numerous of the tribes originally encountered by Spaniards and Anglos. Indians of other tribes blended their cultures more or less peacefully with the white. Nor was the Apache side of the struggle without honor and admirable intentions.

These two men, young and old, present facial features typical of Chiricahua Indians, the best known of all the Apache tribes. Nachez, son of the famous chief Cochise, was in his thirties when this sketch appeared. Nana, head man of the Warm Springs band, was over seventy (*Century,* 1887).

The son of Mangus Colorado, a leader in the last Indian war, 1885-1886 (*Harper's Weekly*, 1886).

"Surprised by a Party of Mexicans," a sketch by Remington (*Outing*, 1887).

JOHN R. BARTLETT, Mexican Boundary Commissioner in 1853, met the Chiricahua and wrote, "They all had a treacherous, fiendish look, which well expressed their true character" but added "Mangus Colorado, and a few other prominent chiefs are rather good looking. . . ."

Apache headdress and boots (Bartlett, 1854).

Apache warrior with a bow (Miles, 1896).

A group of Chiricahua sketched by J. R. Bartlett (Bartlett, 1854).

An Apache family in their finest buckskin dress (*Century,* 1887). Apache tribal classifications are still difficult to understand; the Chiricahua had three bands: the Chiricahua proper, the Warm Springs people, and a southern band. The Tonto, Pinaleño, Coyotero, and Aravaipa have been classed as one tribe, the Western Apache. Early writers also labeled some totally unrelated tribes as Apache, such as the "Yavapai-Apache" and "Mojave-Apache."

Richard Kern, an artist with the Sitgreaves expedition in 1851, drew this curious picture which he called "Yampai Indians." They were probably Yavapai (Sitgreaves, 1853).

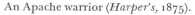

An Apache warrior (*Harper's,* 1875).

R H Kern del

Above, a typical Apache brush shelter in a rancheria or camp (*Harper's Weekly*, 1886). Left, an Apache on the White Mountain reservation (Beadle, 1873). Right, a Remington sketch titled simply "Apache" (*Century*, 1889).

BESIDES the Western Apache and the Chiricahua bands, there were several eastern Apache tribes, notably the Mescalero of New Mexico. It is thought that all these nomads were originally pushed into the far Southwest by the more warlike Comanche, and their language, Athapaskan, is similar to that of modern Iroquois of Canada, the country from which they presumably migrated a thousand or more years ago. The arrival of the Apache in Arizona, however, was quite late, probably not until the beginning of the eighteenth century. Although they are not technically a *rancheria* people (they did not live in scattered villages at permanent agricultural sites), the typical camp of Arizona Apache Indians was usually called a rancheria, and by the nineteenth century they had adopted agriculture in a small way.

One of the largest and most remote of Western Apache bands, the Tonto (Spanish for fools), so-called by Spaniards because the Tonto were ignorant of neighboring Indians and professed to be unable to understand any but their own Athapaskan dialect.

The Tonto Apache boys above, sketched in 1886 by John R. Chapin, bear a striking resemblance to the Tonto at right, sketched by H. B. Möllhausen in 1853 (Outing, 1886; and Whipple, 1855).

A Tonto warrior with his lance, a favorite weapon long after other Apache had adopted firearms (Miles, 1896).

Remington sketch of an Apache woman at San Carlos (*Century*, 1889).

Woman with the distinctive Apache cradleboard (Conklin, 1878).

Apache woman carrying water in a pitch-covered basket on the San Carlos reservation (*Outing*, 1887).

THE WESTERN APACHE BANDS in the first three-quarters of the nineteenth century dominated Arizona from the San Pedro River Valley on the south to the Little Colorado on the north, and from the Blue River near the New Mexican border on the east to the Verde River Valley on the west, roughly one-quarter of modern Arizona. In 1873 they were subdued by General George Crook. A condition of the Apache surrender was that they settle peacefully on the White Mountain and San Carlos reservations, which together comprise over 5,000 square miles in east central Arizona.

Distribution of the beef ration at San Carlos Agency, sketched by Remington in 1888. Note the Scout with the rifle (*Century*, 1889).

An Apache man playing the peculiar one-string fiddle, and a woman carrying a typical Apache basket (*Century*, 1887).

ALTHOUGH APACHE HISTORY remained turbulent until the last Indian war in 1886, the majority of the Western Apache assimilated with other minor tribes such as the Yavapai and remain to this day on their reservations that are considered among the most valuable in the U.S. The White Mountain and San Carlos Indians now number about ten thousand.

An Apache bride (Miles, 1896).

THE FIRST NATIVE DWELLERS to greet the white men were the agricultural Pima and Papago of the Gila and Santa Cruz River valleys who readily accepted features of Spanish life. They were the first to receive reservations from the U.S. government, and to this day they occupy much of the land of their ancestors in the Gila Valley and west of the Santa Cruz in southern Arizona. From the beginning of white contact, the Pima villages near Sacaton were a welcome stopping place on the east-west trail where travelers could obtain food and recruit stock. The Papago along the Santa Cruz, who also are Piman speakers, warred against the Apache.

A Pima couple (Bartlett, 1854).

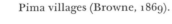

Pima villages (Browne, 1869).

A Papago woman laden with baskets (Roberts, 1885).

Antonio Azul, chief of the Pima in the 1860s and 1870s. In 1872-1873 he led some of his warriors in company with U.S. soldiers against the Apache (Dunn, 1886).

Group of Pima women (Bartlett, 1854).

Pima house construction, using saguaro stalks and grass (Bartlett, 1854).

Captain José, Papago chief who kept whites off his reservation in the 1870s (Browne, 1869).

THE PIMA ARE FAMOUS for their fine basketry, of which large examples were used to store wheat, corn, and other crops grown in irrigated fields. Every summer they also harvested the fruit of the giant saguaro and the beans of the mesquite tree.

Pima "hampta" or large storage bin for grain (Browne, 1874). Below, interior of a thatched hut with several hamptas, squashes, and pumpkins (Bartlett, 1854).

Pima men amusing themselves shooting arrows at a saguaro (Bartlett, 1854).

Pima girls with wicker carriers (Browne, 1869).

Top, a large Pima storage basket (Browne, 1869), and an array of Pima baskets (Bartlett, 1854).

Two scenes in the Coco-Maricopa villages, drawn by W. H. Thwaites from Bartlett's sketches. View at right shows woman weaving a blanket from native cotton (Bartlett, 1854). These Indians are Yuman speakers who moved up from the Colorado to live with the Pima.

THE NOTED Indian portraitist, John Mix Stanley, accompanied the army down the Gila in 1846. In November Stanley's party, under Colonel William H. Emory, camped nine miles above the Pima villages and soon were visited by scores of Indians loaded with corn, beans, honey, and watermelons. After a brisk trade, the party went into the villages where the main body of troops had camped. The Maricopa, Emory stated, were frank and confident in manner, in "strange contrast with that of the suspicious Apache." The Pima he described as a "peaceful and industrious race," possessed "of a beautiful and fertile basin." Stanley took the opportunity to sketch the Pima head chief and a woman interpreter.

A Coco-Maricopa woman, married to a Pima. She served as interpreter to Col. William H. Emory (Emory, 1848).

Juan Antonio, head chief of the Pima, dressed in an army blouse. It was probably the gift of Colonel Emory or General Kearny (Emory, 1848).

Yuma Indians sketched by J. Ross Browne after they received their federal annuity of goods from Arizona's first superintendent of Indian affairs, C. D. Poston, near Yuma in 1864 (Browne, 1869).

Yuma woman grinding corn on a stone metate (James, 1906).

A group of Yuma Indians (Hamilton, 1884).

Two portraits of Pasqual, principal leader of the Yuma from 1854 until his death in 1887. He is shown as a youth in the Woodburytype at left (Campion, 1878) and as an old man in the wood engraving above (Bishop, 1888).

THE YUMA INDIANS and their relatives, the Mojave and Cocopa, occupied the Colorado River Valley from its mouth to the Grand Canyon. The Yuma lived around the confluence of the Gila and Colorado near Yuma, the modern city that bears their name. Acquisitive in the white man's way, they ran a profitable ferry business for emigrants until the 1860s.

A more modern Yuma house, pictured by George Wharton James in 1906.

Yuma house construction sketched in the 1880s (*Century*, 1887).

The Mojave Indians, sketched here by R. H. Kern in 1851, lived north of the Yuma in the Parker Valley and Mojave Valley (Sitgreaves, 1854).

H. B. Möllhausen sketched these Mojave in 1854 at Beale's Crossing on the Colorado, near present-day Davis Dam (Whipple, 1856).

A group of Mojave at Fort Mojave, with an officer's wife in the 1860s (Bell, 1870).

Irataba, chief of the Mojave (Dunn, 1886).

A Mojave dwelling, in a much-copied sketch by Möllhausen (Whipple, 1855).

THE MOJAVE were best known for their elaborate tatoos, rafts (which Lieutenant Whipple used on his expedition in 1854), and basketry. Perennially at war with their relatives, the Walapai (Hualpai) and Chemehuevi, they were generally friendly with the whites and provided some scouts for the army. Today they occupy reservations in their homeland.

A typical Mojave couple (Whipple, 1855).

Mojave runners with the army in the 1880s (Miles, 1896).

Möllhausen's drawing of Irataba, Whipple's guide in 1854; Cairook, chief of the Mojave until his death in 1859; and an unidentified woman, perhaps Cairook's wife. (Whipple, 1855).

Walapai Indians, by H. B. Möllhausen. Note the bows, Apache-style moccasins, and skin garments. A lithograph from Whipple's *Report*, 1855.

A Paiute village in southern Utah sketched by Thomas Moran for John Wesley Powell's narrative, probably drawn from a photograph. Note conical baskets (Powell, 1875).

A "Digger Indian" of southern Nevada (Brewerton, 1854).

OTHER RIVER PEOPLE of the early nineteenth century were the Chemehuevi, Walapai, and Havasupai. The Chemehuevi are a Shoshonean-speaking tribe that moved into the Colorado Valley north of the Bill Williams River after 1800. They were similar to the Paiute of southern Nevada and sometimes called by that name or were called contemptuously "Digger Indians." But the Chemehuevi people dressed in buckskin garments, farmed, and hunted big game. The Walapai lived in the big bend of the Colorado and after 1866 settled on a reservation near Peach Springs. The Havasupai are a tiny group that has resided in the Grand Canyon since before the eighteenth century.

Chemehuevi child in cradle board (Whipple, 1854).

Chemehuevi Indian with bow (Whipple, 1854).

The Hopi village of Walpi, on the tip of First Mesa, showing walled sheep pens (*Harper's Monthly*, 1875).

DURING THE SPANISH RECONQUEST after the Pueblo revolt of 1680-1692, the Hopi were promised amnesty if they would swear allegiance to King Charles II. The Hopi made peace and reluctantly permitted missionaries again to come, but only one village was converted; and this one, Awatovi, was razed and its population scattered by other Hopi in 1700. For another century Spanish policy vacillated between threats and help. Three centuries of white association had passed, yet little white culture had been accepted before the Anglo-Americans came.

THE MOST CULTURALLY ADVANCED of Arizona Indians first contacted by white men were the Hopi, who live today around their three mesas in northeastern Arizona much as they did when first seen by Captain Pedro de Tovar in 1540. The Spaniards called the region "Tusayan." Always a close-knit village society, all the villages except Oraibi until 1681 were in the valleys that dissect the mesas. After the revolt of the New Mexican pueblos in 1680, the Hopi moved the principal villages up onto the mesa tops.

Hopi Chief Yellow Wolf, drawn by artist Edward Kern with a military expedition in 1849 (Simpson, 1850).

Interior of a house in Oraibi (Conklin, 1878).

Below, Na-Ji, a citizen of Mishongnovi (*U.S. Census*, 1890).

IN 1750 THE HOPI numbered nearly eight thousand. By 1850 the population was perhaps 2,500 distributed in a few villages: Walpi, Sichomovi, and Hano on First Mesa; Shongopovi and Mishongnovi on Second Mesa; and Oraibi on Third Mesa. Hano was occupied by descendants of Tewa Indians who had taken refuge there after the Pueblo Revolt of 1680.

A group of Hopi (Beadle, 1873).

An unmarried Hopi girl

Loloma, headman of Oraibi
(*U.S. Census*, 1890).

A courtyard in Walpi (Dellenbaugh, 1904).

A Tewa woman of Hano. The hair style with two circular ropes on the sides is called "squash blossom" and is worn only by unmarried girls. From a sketch by Julian Scott (*U.S. Census*, 1890).

Right, view of Shongopovi showing entrance to an underground ceremonial chamber called a kiva (Powell, 1895).

Hopi Snake Dance
(Higgins, 1895).

MOST PICTURESQUE of all Hopi ceremonials is the Snake Dance performed each summer before the rainy season. This is only one Hopi rite, performed by the Snake Clan. All clans have distinctive ceremonies to bring rain and ensure full crops, but the Snake Dance is spectacular because it dispenses with symbols and uses live rattlesnakes.

Dance court and Dance Rock at the Hopi pueblo of Walpi (Lummis, 1892).

"Praying for rain" was the artist's title for this picture in 1885, in a Hopi village. Rain ceremonies are found in all pueblos. Hopi families that had lived for a time at Zuni pueblo brought back Zuni religious ceremonies and the crafts of pottery and silverwork (Gleed, 1885).

Street in the ghost town of Awatovi. (Beadle, 1873).

Distant view of Mishongnovi, a Second Mesa town (Powell, 1895).

"Hopi" is a contraction of the Indians' name for themselves, from "Hopituh" or "the peaceful ones." Until the twentieth century white men called them by the name given by the Spaniards: "Moqui," "Mohoce," or "Mohoqui," probably a rendition of the name of one of the prehistoric villages in the Jadito Valley. Oraibi ("the rock") is the oldest continuously occupied town in the United States, the Hopi having built on Third Mesa before fear of Spaniard and Navajo drove them up the other mesas.

A passageway in Mishongnovi (Powell, 1895).

"Moquis Pueblos," lithograph from a sketch by F. W. von Egloffstein, the German cartographer with Lieutenant J. C. Ives' expedition, who made this view of Second Mesa in 1858 (Ives, 1861).

"Snake Dance of the Moquis" by A. F. Harmer. This early example of photolithography was made by the London firm of C. F. Kell in 1884. Harmer, an army sergeant, accompanied Captain John G. Bourke to Walpi in the summer of 1881. On August 12 they witnessed the public part of the Snake Clan ritual, and Harmer made a careful pencil sketch which Bourke used to illustrate his classic work on the subject, *The Snake-Dance of the Moquis of Arizona* (New York, 1884). (Compare this artist's version with the engraving made from a photograph on p. 26.)

A Hopi man spinning with the spindle underfoot, revolved by his foot and the wheel-like whorl (BAE, 1882).

UNLIKE THE NAVAJO, the Hopi are not great stock raisers, but they early accepted sheep and goats from the Spaniards and learned to spin and weave wool. Weaving is man's work, done on an upright loom secured on two posts in the ground.

Below, the house of Talti, chief of the town council in Old Oraibi, from a drawing by Thomas Moran (Powell, 1895).

HOPI KACHINA DOLLS are skilfully carved by the men from cottonwood roots and represent both the dancers who celebrate the feast of bean planting and the gods themselves, who are said to dwell on the San Francisco Mountain peaks. The feast, celebrated in March, is the Hopi equivalent of Christmas, and the dolls are given to children.

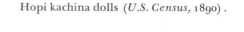

Hopi kachina dolls (*U.S. Census*, 1890).

A scene in Hano, the town begun by Tewa Indian refugees after the Pueblo Revolt in 1680. Although Hopi in all other respects, the Hano villagers still speak their Tewa dialect (Powell, 1895).

Entrance to a kiva, foreground, at Old Oraibi, from a sketch by Thomas Moran (Powell, 1895).

Hopi women dressing
their hair
(BAE, 1882).

The Hopi village of Walpi,
which means "place of the
gap" (Lummis, 1892).

INTERSPERSED with the pueblo peoples—the Hopi and the Zuni of New Mexico—were the Navajo who roamed westward into Arizona, at times as far as Kaibab Creek in the early nineteenth century. Today they occupy the largest reservation in Arizona, the entire northeast corner of the state except for the Hopi enclave. They are also the largest Indian tribe in the United States. Over 110,000 Navajo live on their Arizona-New Mexico-Colorado preserve. Their population and the extent of their home in Arizona, however, is largely a modern development, for in the last century the Navajo, Athapaskan kin of the Apache, were nomadic raiders in northern New Mexico, southern Colorado, and Utah. Their early history is really more a part of New Mexico where perhaps 3,000 preyed on the Rio Grande settlements and the eastern pueblos. After Anglo-American occupation of New Mexico in 1846, five military expeditions entered the Navajo country; and in 1849 Colonel J. M. Washington, military governor of New Mexico, succeeded in making a treaty with some of them at Bear Springs near Chinle, west of the Navajo stronghold of Canyon de Chelly in Arizona.

Chapaton, chief of the San Juan band of Navajo. He made peace in 1849 at Canyon de Chelly and was shortly afterward murdered by Mexicans near Ciboletta, New Mexico. Lithograph by Edward Kern after a sketch by his brother Richard (Simpson, 1850).

Valley of Fort Defiance in 1858 (Ives, 1861).

THE WARLIKE NAVAJO were never subdued by the Spaniards or Mexicans. Even the U.S. Army failed in its first attempt in 1859, and the Navajo united to drive whites from their land. Their attack on Fort Defiance, repulsed with bloody loss, was the only attack by Indians on an army post in Arizona. Peace might have ensued but the Navajo were again encouraged when most army posts were abandoned at the start of the Civil War.

Canyon de Chelly in the Navajo country, now a National Monument (*Century,* 1890).

An early Navajo warrior (Dunn, 1886).

Spider Rock in Canyon de Chelly. "Spider Woman" lives on top and descends to carry off bad children (Beadle, 1873).

Navajo ready for a journey (Powell, 1895).

A typical early Navajo blanket, good enough for rough use (BAE, 1882).

A woman at her loom, bringing down the batten (BAE, 1882).

Navajo blanket of fine quality (BAE, 1882).

The great war chief of the Navajo was Manuelito (c.1819-1894), whose son Manuelito Segundo is portrayed in his finest costume (woodcut after a photo, Conklin, 1878).

Among Navajo, the women spin and weave. (BAE, 1882)

Navajo weaver at work outside a modern hogan. (BAE, 1882)

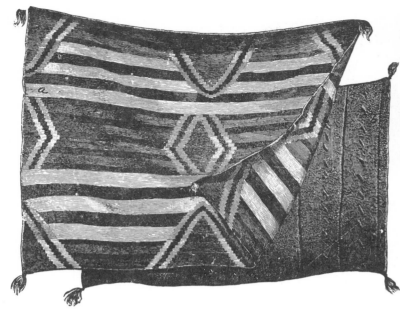

Three Navajo blankets: above left. a "bayeta" blanket of the so-called "chief" design, over one of flannel. Above right, a blanket of native wool. "Bayeta" is Spanish for baize, the woolen material imported into the Navajo country in the nineteenth century. From it Navajo women respun yarn of long, fine, continuous strands for weaving the finest blankets (all from James, 1914).

NAVAJO HISTORY from 1861 to 1868 involved the Long Walk and other events as crucial to them as the War between the States is to Anglo-Americans. An initial treaty settled 400 Navajo at Fort Sumner on the Pecos River. The vast majority preferred war. Kit Carson invaded Canyon de Chelly and convinced 8,000 to surrender. Only 23 were killed and 200 captured; the rest drifted in to Fort Defiance for safety, warmth, and food.

A special loom for belt weaving, with a saddle girth in progress. The small comb at lower left marked (a) is a device used sometimes to pound the weft (BAE, 1882).

Loom details: the warp (i-i) is strung between beams f and k, then hung from the crossbeam (b) with an adjustable stick between (d). The upright supports (a-a) and lower beam (hidden) must be rigid. Unless the rug is to be small, extra warp must be rolled under for later use (h). Items m and n are heald rods, and l is the batten with which the weaver brings down the weft (BAE, 1882).

KIT CARSON'S TROOPS escorted large groups
of Navajo to the Bosque Redondo reservation on the Pecos on the Long Walk. 2,000
died there in 1865; 7,300 survived until
President Grant's Peace Commission signed
a treaty with them in 1868. This gave them
a reservation in Arizona and the promise of
schools, agricultural tools, and livestock.

8: 52   JĀN BÎK'EHGO HANE'-YA'AT'É'HI   9: 7

diṡnîh, t'a-ḥai'-dah ła' dîneh
sād beh yaṡti'igi yāahalyāṅ-
go ėi do anîneh yîdołtsėł'
dah.

52 Ako Juz anādahodo'nid,
K'adt nîḣił bė'dahozîn nîł-
c'iḥ-bī-ini'zini niyî'di holoṅ
laṅh', Ėbraham îndah ahodoni'łi-yadahalne'i ėi daneznah', ako nîḣ adinîh, T'a-
ḥai'-dah sād beh yaṡti'igi
yāahalyaṅgo ėi do anîneh
yîdo'lîṅh' dah.

53 Da' ni'iṡ nîḣiła Ėbraham
yēnî' ėi daztsan'îgi bîlāhgo
ant'eh ? ahodoni'łi-yadahalne'i ałdo' daneznah': akoṡaṅ'
hai i'dîl'iṅh?

54 Jesus anādo'nid, T'a ṡîh
ayoanîṡt'eh i'dîṡyago ako
ayoanîṡt'ėhîgi do i'liṅ' dah
dolėł; ṡîła ėi ayoat'ė'i ṡėidiāh,
nîḣi God at'eh dadohnîn'îgi :

Ėbraham t'a bîtsė'daṅ honiṡ-
łoṅh.

59 A'kohgo tseh ṅi'dadzizlā
beh dahwiżdołnił' bîniyeh,
ṅidîh Jeṡus hats'aṅ ṅi'des-
t'iṅ, ado bī-sohodîzîn-kîn bi-
yî'do c'iżniyah, ado bîłahgo
c'iżniyah, ado yo'ajiyah.

WOLTA'I 9.

1 Ado Jesus t'a a'kwi jo-
gał'go dîneh ła' t'a bîdîżcîn-
deṅ bînā at'dîn lė'i dzîł-
tsaṅh.

2 Ako hodahoł'āhîgi ṅida-
hodeł'kît, Na'ntîni, hai'ṡaṅ'
baṅhîgi a'dzah, di dîneh dats'i, haṡci'ni dats'i ako t'a ha-
nā at'dingo hodîżcîṅh?

3 Jesus ahodi'nid, Di dîneh
do baṅhîgi a'dza dah, ado
bîṡcîn'îgi ałdo' dodah: ṅidîh
God yanagāhîgi beh bė'ho-

A page from the Bible printed in Navajo
orthography, devised by the Franciscan fathers
at Fort Defiance (American Bible Society,
1918).

The traditional Navajo dwelling called
a "hogan," partly dug into the earth
(Powell, 1895).

The colorful ritual Fire Dance of the Navajo
(Powell, 1895).

II. THE LAND

The Chiricahua Mountains loom above the San Simon Valley where the Boundary Commission camped (Bartlett, 1854).

ARIZONA LANDSCAPE.

The stinging grass and thorny plants
  And all its prickly tropic glories,
The thieving, starved inhabitants,
  Who look so picturesque in stories.

The dusty, long, hot, dreary way,
  Where 'neath a blazing sun you totter,
To reach a camp at close of day
  And find it destitute of water.

The dying mule, the dried-up spring,
  Which novel writers seldom notice;
The song the blood mosquitoes sing,
  And midnight howling of coyotes.

Tarantulas and centipedes,
  Horn'd toads and piercing mezquit daggers,
With thorny bushes, grass and weeds
  To bleed the traveler as he staggers.

Why paint things in a rosy light,
  And never tell the simple fact thus—
How one sits down to rest at night,
  And ofter squats upon a cactus?

An early poetic tribute (Beadle, 1873).

The Dragoon Mountain fastness where Chiricahua Indians hid in the "Cochise Stronghold" (Miles, 1896).

Charles F. Lummis called southern Arizona "The Great American Desert." It is, in fact, part of the Sonoran Desert (Lummis, 1892).

The Santa Rita Valley was the name of the opening in the Santa Rita Mountains pictured above by
H. C. Grosvenor, a wood engraver turned mine manager who was murdered here by the Apache in 1861.
The hills on the south side of the valley now bear Grosvenor's name (Pumpelly, 1870).

Mount Graham may have been named for any one of five persons; the question remains unsettled. With an
elevation of 10,720 feet, it is the highest peak in southern Arizona. The range it dominates is sometimes called
the Graham Mountains, and early settlers called them the Sierra Bonitas, but they are properly the Pinaleños
(Emory, 1848).

The jagged horn of Baboquivari Peak, elevation 7,730 feet. It is sacred to the Indians and marks the eastern boundary of the Papago Reservation (Browne, 1868) .

The canyon of Aravaipa Creek, heading north from Sulphur Springs Valley and then west into the San Pedro River. The canyon was site of the Camp Grant Massacre, 1871. Lithographed from a photograph (Bell, 1870) .

THERE ARE FOUR major geographic divisions to Arizona. For simplicity the state is often divided between the north and the south, into the drainages of the Gila River and the mighty Colorado. Actually, the plateau country drained by the Colorado River and the Basin-and-Range Province (as geographers call the southwestern half of Arizona) are only two chief divisions. There is also a mountain zone at the edge of the Colorado Plateau and a transition zone below the Mogollon Rim which traverses the state diagonally. The south is characterized by 150 island-like mountain ranges—such as the Chiricahua, Catalina, Mohawk, and Kofa—generally trending from northwest to southeast and separated by expanses of true desert. In the west some of the basins drain directly into the Colorado rather than the Gila. Travelers readily distinguish as well a region of grassy prairies in southeastern Arizona, though it is still technically a part of the vast Basin-and-Range Province and the larger Sonoran Desert.

The Tinajas Altas ("high tanks"), 40 miles south-east of Yuma, as drawn by Carl Schuchard. They supplied precious water on the dangerous desert trail called "El Camino del Diablo" (Gray, 1856).

THE ECOLOGICAL ZONES of Arizona are largely determined by elevation. Yuma receives little more than three inches of rain a year, the San Francisco Mountains get as much as 23, and the state average is but seven. Aridity is the common factor.

A view of Salt River Canyon (Emory, 1848).

ABOUT FORTY-TWO PER CENT of Arizona, ranging up to 5,000 feet, is covered by creosote bush, sagebrush, mesquite, ironwood, and cacti. Twenty-three per cent of Arizona land, ranging between 3,200 and 6,500 feet in elevation, is grassland. Woodlands are scattered; those extending southeast from Bill Williams Mountain to the Blue River cover more than 10,000 square miles.

Coronation Peak in the Muggins Mountains, 20 miles northeast of Yuma. It was a landmark on the trail to California. Spanish explorers likened it to a mitred crown; Bartlett called it Pagoda Mountain (Bartlett, 1854).

Below, the volcanic cone called Artillery Peak, 30 miles east of Parker Dam and on the north side of Bill Williams River. (Whipple, 1856).

The Hassayampa River, of doubtful Spanish name, flows past Wickenburg to the Gila. It is shown here at Walnut Grove, about twenty miles from Wickenburg. An old poem says, "Those who drink its water bright / Red man, white man, boor, or knight / Girls or women, boys or men, / Never can tell the truth again" (*Scribner's,* 1890).

THE MOUNTAIN ZONE of central and eastern Arizona is 6,500 to 9,000 feet high. The San Francisco Mountains rise over 12,000 feet, with alpine meadows surrounded by dense pine forest. In the south, higher mountains such as the Pinaleños and Catalinas also are forested. More characteristic of Arizona, however, are the piñon and juniper woodlands that cover nearly a fifth of the state. And the most varied of the vegetation zones is the chaparral, a mixed brushland that thrives everywhere between 4,000 and 5,500 feet.

View of the Santa Maria Mountains across the valley of Walnut Creek. Explorers called it "Aztec Pass" for ruins nearby (Whipple, 1856).

An artist with Whipple paused on the south side of the Chino Valley to sketch Black Mesa and Picacho Butte, ten miles southeast of Seligman. Whipple named this region "the Black Forest" (Whipple, 1856).

Below, the Whipple expedition camped near the modern town of Williams, and their report included this view of the Bill Williams Mountain. The peak is 9,264 feet high and was named for the legendary mountain man and guide who passed this way many times (Whipple, 1861).

Castle Dome on the Colorado, forty miles northeast of Yuma. Silver and lead were mined here in the 1860s (Browne, 1869).

A herd of antelope and The Needles, five miles south of Topock, as drawn by Möllhausen in 1853. The name of the three sharp peaks was used for an Arizona town and later for a California city (Möllhausen, 1861).

Colorado River below the railroad bridge at Topock (James, 1906).

Mount Whipple, now called Grossman Peak, in the Mohave Mountains south of The Needles (Ives, 1861).

SOME FEATURES of Arizona topography are unique. The Colorado River and its valley are in this class, though modern dam building and the siphoning of its waters to California have destroyed some of the most striking attributes. The stream rises in Grand County, Colorado and flows southwest through Colorado, Utah, Arizona, and briefly Mexico before emptying into the Gulf of California. It includes the stream formerly known as the North Fork of Grand River, and when so defined is about 1,400 miles in length. Another oddity is the Petrified Forest, fifteen miles east of Holbrook. Here, perhaps 200 million years ago, volcanic ash covered more than 80,000 acres of trees which turned to stone before the cover eroded.

View in Petrified Forest (Higgins, 1911).

Petrified Forest (Miles, 1896).

Silicified tree in Lithodendron Wash (Whipple, 1856).

Stoneman Lake, a water-filled crater thirty miles south of Flagstaff, was named for the commander of the Arizona military department who was later California's governor (Hinton, 1878).

Tonto Natural Bridge, eighty miles below Flagstaff, was built by deposit from limestone springs. It is nearly 400 feet wide (Lummis, 1892).

The canyon of Bill Williams River, or the Santa Maria as it is known in its upper reach. The trapper for whom it is named explored much of northern Arizona and probably took many beaver here (Whipple, 1856).

THE GRAND CANYON of the Colorado is considered by many to be the greatest natural wonder in the world. Not merely is it a stupendous chasm a mile deep and four to eighteen miles wide, but it is also an open book of geologic history. It is Arizona cross-sectioned, with Kaibab snows at the top and Sonoran desert at the bottom. Its varicolored strata exhibit time from Pre-Cambrian to the present. Embayed rims and fantastic monuments to erosion stretch far away and into the depths, catching sunlight or shadow with dramatic beauty.

Thomas Moran drew this picture of Grand Canyon looking west from Toroweap Point (Powell, 1875).

A spectacular valley on the eastern edge of the Chiricahua Mountains was also called a "grand canyon" (Gray, 1856).

The Grand Canyon from the brink of the inner gorge, from a Moran picture (Powell, 1875).

Tourists reach the bottom of the Grand Canyon via Bright Angel Trail (*Harper's Monthly*, 1898).

Below, Grand Canyon as seen from Point Sublime (*Harper's Monthly*, 1890).

The 12,670-foot Humphreys Peak in the San Francisco Mountains is the highest point in Arizona, named for Gen. Andrew A. Humphreys (Powell, 1895).

Volcanic cinder cones east of the San Francisco Mountains, as portrayed in the report of the Ives expedition (Ives, 1861).

"Glen Canyon" was perhaps the best wood engraving made from a Moran painting (Bryant, 1874).

Mouth of the Little Colorado. All views on this page are from drawings by Thomas Moran (Powell, 1875).

A highly romanticized sketch of Sentinel Rock in Grand Canyon (Powell, 1875).

Aspen forest near Flagstaff (Steele, 1890).

Mount Trumbull, above, 8,028 feet high, overlooks Toroweap Valley leading south from the Uinkaret Plateau to the Grand Canyon (Powell, 1895).

A distant view of the San Francisco Peaks from the north, as pictured by an artist with the Ives Expedition (Ives, 1861).

ARIZONA'S NORTHEAST CORNER is Indian country, and the land of the Hopi and the Navajo presents wild extremes of topography—the Little Colorado River, the Canyon de Chelly, the Painted Desert, and numerous mesas and plateaus. Largely high desert, Indian country includes the Chuska Mountains extending into New Mexico.

"The Thousand Wells," a region of natural reservoirs near House Rock Valley (Shearer, 1884).

Spruce forests on the Navajo Reservation (Beadle, 1873).

The San Francisco Mountains as seen by Richard Kern from a camp east of Flagstaff (Sitgreaves, 1854).

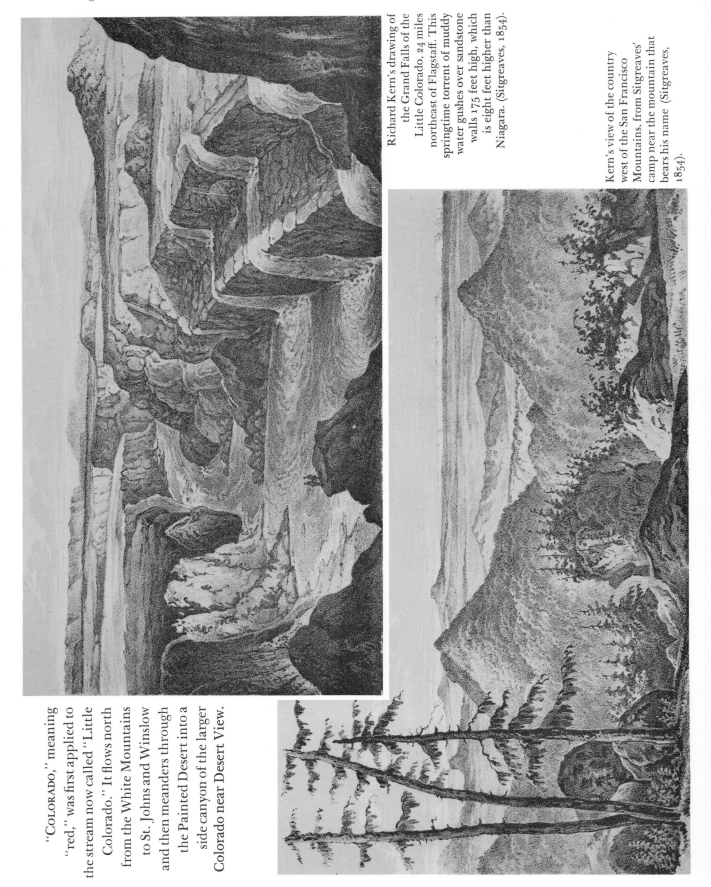

"COLORADO," meaning "red," was first applied to the stream now called "Little Colorado." It flows north from the White Mountains to St. Johns and Winslow and then meanders through the Painted Desert into a side canyon of the larger Colorado near Desert View.

Richard Kern's drawing of the Grand Falls of the Little Colorado, 24 miles northeast of Flagstaff. This springtime torrent of muddy water gushes over sandstone walls 175 feet high, which is eight feet higher than Niagara. (Sitgreaves, 1854).

Kern's view of the country west of the San Francisco Mountains, from Sitgreaves' camp near the mountain that bears his name (Sitgreaves, 1854).

Canyon de Chelly shown in a lithograph made from a photograph taken by Lieutenant George M. Wheeler in 1873. The sandstone column at right is Spider Rock; compare this view with that shown on page 34. The black and white reproduction above is weak compared to the magnificent colors of the original print (Wheeler, 1889).

Three prominent types of cactus, below (Bishop, 1888). The giant saguaro symbolizes the region; its bloom is the state flower. The tree-like, ugly cholla attaches painful thorns to the unwary hiker. The bush-like maguey provides food and fiber; tequila is distilled from its roots.

There are more varieties of rattlesnakes in Arizona than in any other state (*Century*, 1889).

The Gila monster. It is the only poisonous lizard and is found only in Arizona and parts of Mexico. Fortunately it is very shy and is today protected by law (*Century*, 1889).

A dense stand of cactus (Sidney, 1886).

Grizzly bears—the big silvertips—roamed Arizona until the end of the nineteenth century (*Century,* 1891).

Barrel cactus, showing two smaller species and a larger variety (Kent, 1890).

Climbing from the Grand Canyon (Powell, 1875).

The roadrunner, a strange and comical bird that rarely flies but can run 30 miles an hour. It fearlessly attacks rattlesnakes (*Hutchings',* 1856).

Juniper trees, right, so impressed Richard Kern that he drew them larger than life (Sitgreaves, 1854). The mountains of central Arizona with altitudes between 5,000 and 7,000 feet are dotted with the dwarf pine called piñon and several types of juniper or rough-barked cedar trees.

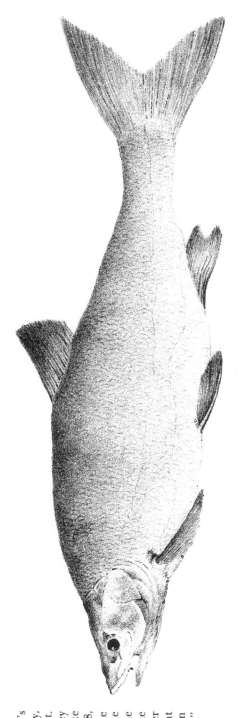

Gila trout, right, Arizona's most distinctive fish (Emory, 1848). It is now nearly extinct. "At first it was supposed they were mountain trout," wrote Lieutenant Emory in 1848. "but . . . I soon saw the difference . . . at a little distance, you will imagine the fish covered with delicate scales, but on closer examination you will find that they are only the impression of scales."

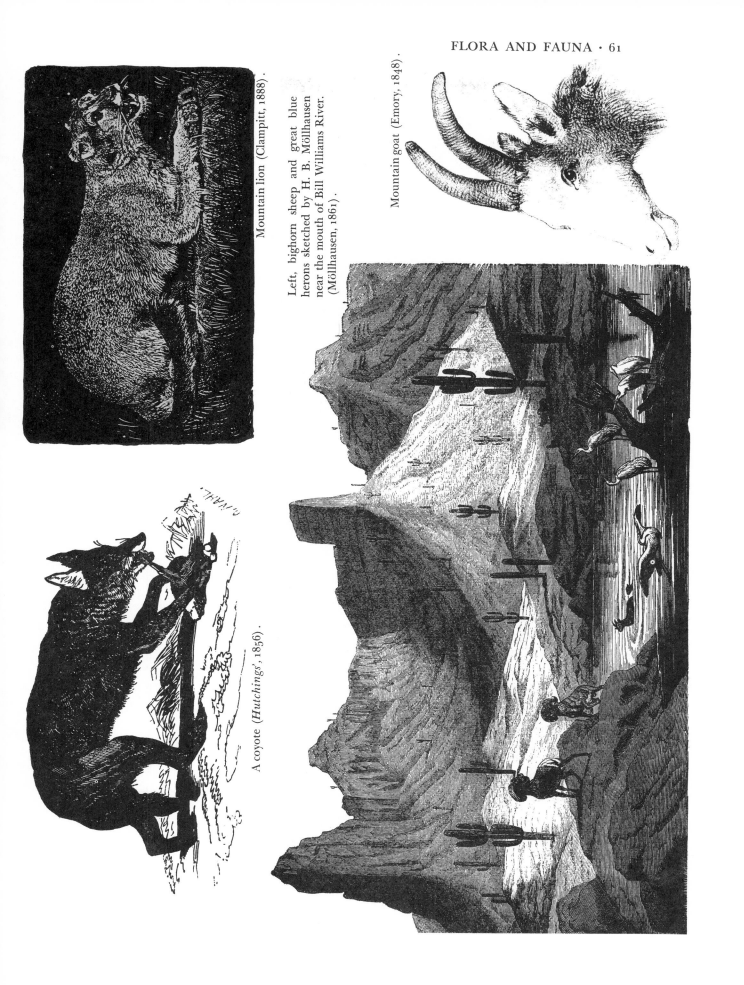

Mountain lion (Clampitt, 1888).

Left, bighorn sheep and great blue herons sketched by H. B. Möllhausen near the mouth of Bill Williams River. (Möllhausen, 1861).

Mountain goat (Emory, 1848).

A coyote (Hutchings', 1856).

Mesquite branch
(James, 1906).

Möllhausen's lithographic view of Chimney Peak on the California side of the Colorado, about 18 miles above Yuma. The herd of elk may be artistic license as they are far from their usual home in the mountains of central Arizona (Möllhausen, 1861).

A "horned toad," really a lizard, drawn life size (Elliott, 1884).

THE STUDY OF NATURAL HISTORY was greatly advanced by scientists who accompanied the army explorers, but few realistic pictures of wildlife found their way into popular books. Möllhausen's 1861 account of his Arizona adventures, published in German, was an exception. After helping to illustrate Whipple's railroad survey and Ives' Colorado River report, Möllhausen gave his best work to his Leipzig publisher.

Mesquite trees
(James, 1906).

Black-tailed deer
(Connelley, 1907).

ROBERTS SC.

Yucca plant,
larger than life, and elk
(Whipple, 1856).

"Vegetation of the High
Plateaus" by Möllhausen.
The black bears and turkeys
are seen amidst oak and
juniper trees. A fox
crouches near a joshua tree
(Möllhausen, 1861).

Mummy Cave and ruined village in Canyon del Muerto (*Century*, 1890).

Right, mound ruins at La Tempe on the Salt River (Bartlett, 1854).

Below, ruined pueblos of Wupatki as seen by R. H. Kern in 1853 near Sunset Crater (Sitgreaves, 1854).

ANOTHER FEATURE of the land that fascinated early travelers was the ubiquitous reminders of prehistoric dwellers. The wonder and amazement of the earliest Anglo explorers upon discovering the ancient ruins inspired an intense interest in archaeology. The very first American anthropologists— William H. Holmes, J. W. Powell, Adolph F. A. Bandelier, and Frederick Webb Hodge —started their investigations in the Southwest, particularly among the prehistoric sites of Arizona. Yet even before then a host of amateurs had discovered nearly all the spectacular ruins. Antonio de Espejo stopped at Montezuma's Well in 1583; the Casa Grande was sketched by Juan Mateo Mange in 1694. Tourism was born early.

MANY ARIZONA cliff houses were built before 1300 A.D. by prehistoric people. Canyon de Chelly was later a Navajo stronghold, and the Indians regarded the spirit dwellings with awe.

A ruined cliff village in Canyon de Chelly (*Century*, 1890).

Montezuma's Well in the Verde Valley (left); note cliff houses below rim (Lummis, 1892). Above, another view of the "well," a limestone sinkhole fed by streams and not a well. It had no connection with Montezuma (Hinton, 1878).

Picknickers in Walnut Canyon near Flagstaff. More than 300 masonry rooms are hidden in the canyon walls (Higgins, 1895).

Planta ichnographica de la Casa grande del Rio Gila.

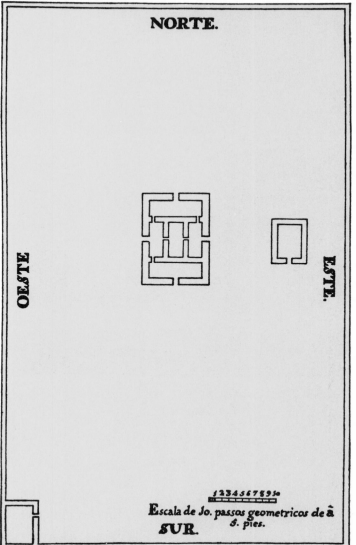

Father Pedro Font's 1775 plan of Casa Grande compound (Bolton, 1933).

WITHOUT DOUBT the most famous prehistoric ruin of Arizona is the great pile of adobe twelve miles west of the modern town of Florence called by the Spaniards the "Casa Grande" (the Great House). The first white man to see the Casa Grande was the Jesuit missionary-explorer Eusebio Kino who said a mass within its walls in 1694. Father Pedro Font, journeying to California, stopped at the ruin in 1775. Nearly every writer concerned with Southwestern history has referred to the Great House on the Gila River, and many others have alluded to its possible connection with Meso-America in discussing the antiquities of Mexico. As one might expect, many of those who wrote in the nineteenth century introduced engraved or lithographed pictures of the ruin. Only a sampling can be shown here.

The Casa Grande is an imposing monument to the past. The standing walls—windowless and wrinkled, unlike any modern pueblo—rise forty feet out of the flat desert. At first the site was attributed to southward migrating ancestors of the Aztec or Toltec, which would be interesting enough if true. By 1912, however, J. W. Fewkes had concluded that there was no foundation for such belief. Yet by then it was also clear that the people who occupied the Casa Grande were no relation either to the ancient Hohokam desert people or the modern Piman speakers.

Below, woodcut of the main Casa Grande ruin (Gleed, 1885).

Design of Casa Grande earthenware bowl, distinctive of the Lower Gila region and also found among Sinagua-Anasazi remains on the Little Colorado (BAE, *28th Ann. Rept., 1906-07*, 1912).

Casa Grande ruins pictured by John Mix Stanley, artist on the Emory reconnaissance (Emory, 1848). The ground enclosures were filled solid with earth to a height of about seven feet. Above this platform two outside stories were erected and the central enclosure had three stories.

Casa Grande sketched by Captain Abraham R. Johnston, who followed Emory. Published in Johnston's *Journal,* issued with Emory's *Notes* (Emory, 1848). Ground plan shows five enclosures. Walls were made of puddled adobe cast in large open forms and moved to successive layers.

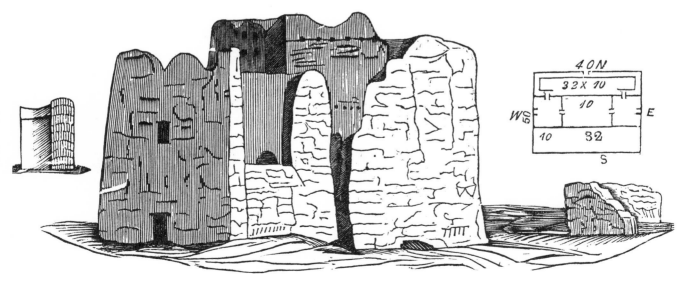

Casa Grande as viewed from the southwest, in a fine lithograph made from a watercolor painting done on the spot by John Russell Bartlett in 1852 (Bartlett, 1854). It shows much of the southwest corner of the compound still standing.

Below, a wood engraving from a sketch by J. Ross Browne (Browne, 1869). It shows the northeast side of Casa Grande. The walls fortunately did not deteriorate much more before the ruin was declared a National Monument in 1918.

THE CASA GRANDE is but one of four blocks of now ruined buildings termed "compound" pueblos by archaeologists. A visitor soon discovers that the Great House stood among half a dozen or more structures, which were surrounded at one time by a wall approximately 420 by 220 feet. Three other compounds and some isolated houses occupied altogether perhaps a quarter section one mile south of the Gila.

Top, left, Cliff House in Canyon de Chelly (Thayer, 1888). A thrill comes from climbing the weathered footholds to a cave dwelling.

Top, right, the White House or Casa Blanca in Canyon de Chelly, in a woodcut that equals modern photographs (*Century*, 1890). This ruin, together with Montezuma's Castle, are the most spectacular cave dwellings in Arizona.

Left, a secluded cliff village in Monument Canyon, which runs into Canyon de Chelly (*Century*, 1890). Fully described by Cosmos Mindeleff in 1897, the ruins were incorporated into a national monument several years later. Mindeleff alone mapped and studied 140 villages in the area, culturally linked with the famous Mesa Verde in Colorado.

Montezuma's Castle seen from the foot of the cliff (Lummis, 1892).

Below, some ruins in the Verde Valley showing the cyclopean type of construction (Hinton, 1878).

Montezuma's Castle as seen from Beaver Creek (Lummis, 1892).

ANOTHER PREHISTORIC RUIN, and nearly as well known as the Casa Grande, is the cliff village fifty miles south of Flagstaff on Beaver Creek, a tributary of the Verde River. The Indians who farmed the bottom of Beaver Creek in the twelfth to the fifteenth centuries and who built the cliff houses now called "Montezuma's Castle" may have been related to those who invaded the Hohokam country along the Gila and built the Great House. After the eruption of Sunset Crater in 1065, new settlers from the east (Anasazi) and from the south (Hohokam) were attracted by the fertility of the volcanic ash. In the twelfth century the Sinagua-Anasazi advanced southward, pushing the Hohokam out of the Verde Valley and about 1250 began to construct homes of masonry in the limestone cliffs high above Beaver Creek. As many as 200 persons may have lived here until the castle was as suddenly abandoned about 1450 as was Casa Grande somewhat earlier.

Four views of carved and painted rocks: above, Browne, 1869; left, Fröbel, 1857; below, Bartlett, 1854; and bottom of page, Gleed, 1882.

ASSOCIATED WITH RUINS but often alone are intriguing prehistoric pictographs. Today it is generally acknowledged that these crude symbols are without conventional meaning, although uncertain as to purpose. Some drawings on rocks may be rude maps of trails and waterholes, but it is fairly certain that Southwestern Indians never came close to evolving an alphabet or intending anything like hieroglyphics. Best known in the last century was the mass of random carvings and paintings on a jumble of boulders called "the Painted Rocks," 65 miles southwest of Phoenix. Bartlett, who had been involved in the controversy over the inscriptions on Dighton Rock in Massachusetts in 1834, took great interest in the Arizona pictographs and made careful copies of some.

Two early versions of the Grand Canyon: above, a wood engraving titled "Vishnu's Temple," probably copied from a photograph (Thayer, 1888). Below, Möllhausen's lithograph "Gorges in the High Plateau and View of the Colorado Canyon" (Möllhausen, 1861).

III. SPANISH AND MEXICAN ARIZONA

Captain Garcia Lopez de Cardenas, guided by Hopi Indians in August of 1540, gazed in disbelief into the Grand Canyon. Deceived by the clear atmosphere, he thought the chasm but a few hundred feet deep and the river at the bottom no more than "a fathom wide," but three of his men required a whole day to descend and return. Maynard Dixon captured this dramatic moment in a little known painting (*Land O'Sunshine,* 1900).

SPANIARDS BROUGHT the first foundations of white European civilization to the American Southwest. Nowhere has the Spanish culture been so deeply ingrained as in southern Arizona and the upper Rio Grande Valley.

Sixteenth-century Spanish soldier armed with harquebus and halberd (Ullastres, 1884).

An early explorer (Steele, 1890).

The standard carried by this Spanish cavalryman is the one Coronado would have had (Ullastres, 1884).

TRADITIONALLY ARIZONA HISTORY begins in 1540 with a bow to Francisco Vasquez de Coronado who may or may not have trod the southeastern valleys. It is more certain that Coronado's partner, Hernando de Alarcon, explored the lower valley of the Rio Colorado, ascending the river in boats perhaps as far as today's Martinez Lake. This was in September. In December the commander of Coronado's rear base on the Sonora River, Melchior Diaz, journeyed west to the site of modern Yuma but failed to meet Alarcon. Also, Coronado's captain, Garcia Lopez de Cardenas, discovered the Grand Canyon while seeking the Colorado River on a tip from Captain Pedro de Tovar who had visited the Hopi mesas in the summer of 1540. Altogether, however, they can scarcely be said to have explored Arizona. Nor was much more accomplished by a private prospecting party led by Antonio de Espejo from New Mexico to the Verde River in 1582. In the winter of 1604-05, Don Juan de Oñate, the conquistador of New Mexico, led an expedition across central Arizona and down the Colorado to its mouth.

A mounted *arcabucero* loading his weapon. Firing the harquebus from horseback would have been dangerous (Ullastres, 1884).

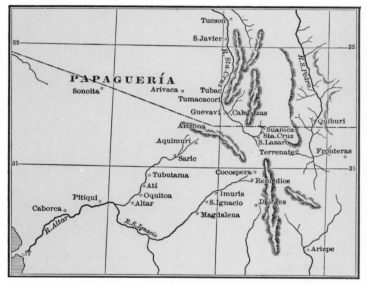

The missions of Arizona (Bancroft, 1889).

FOR NEARLY A CENTURY Arizona lay dormant with only sporadic attention given to the Hopi from Santa Fe. The first successful entry was by Jesuit missionaries, beginning with Father Eusebio Francisco Kino who preached to the Pima at a village he called San Cayetano del Tumacacori in January of 1691.

INEVITABLY THE ESTABLISHMENT of missions was accompanied by that other great civilizing institution of the Spanish Borderlands, the presidios, whose military garrisons founded permanent towns such as Fronteras, Sonora. From his headquarters here in 1736 Captain Juan Bautista de Anza the Elder took troops to keep order and to confiscate the King's share of wealth in a fabulous silver discovery at "Arizonac"—a mining settlement near modern Nogales which gave its name to the state.

First page of the diary of Juan de Anza on his trip across Arizona in 1775-76 (Bolton, 1930).

The town of Fronteras, 25 miles south of Douglas, Arizona, was founded by Juan de Anza in 1692. Here was born his more famous son and namesake who explored Arizona and was governor of New Mexico (Bartlett, 1854).

Spanish helmet of the seventeenth century, a type probably seen in Arizona (Ullastres, 1884).

THE YOUNGER DE ANZA took over the presidio at Tubac, Arizona, in 1760. From there he explored a route to California. In 1775 he followed the Gila Trail across the Colorado and his expedition founded San Francisco in the next year.

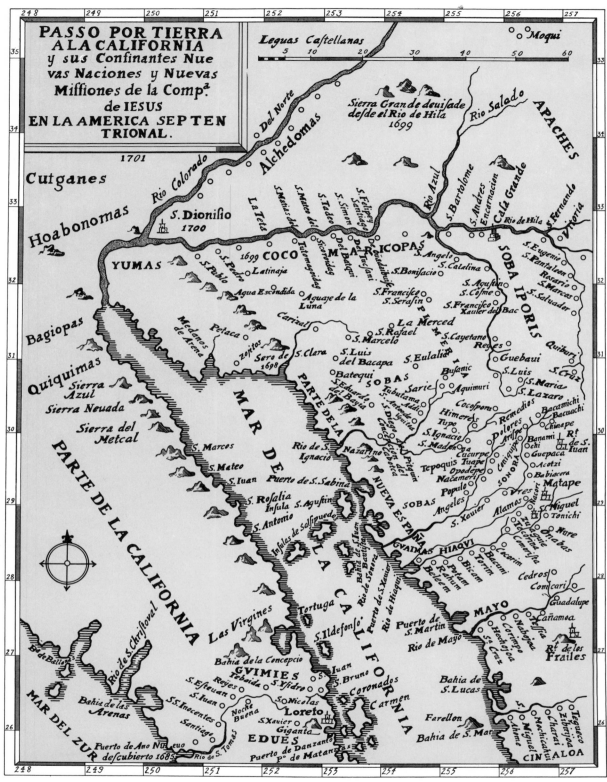

PASSO POR TIERRA A LA CALIFORNIA y sus Confinantes Nue vas Naciones y Nuevas Missiones de la Comp.ª de IESUS EN LA AMERICA SEPTEN TRIONAL.

1701

Leguas Castellanas
5 10 20 30 40 50 60

Moqui

Sierra Grande deuisade desde el Rio de Hila 1699

APACHES

Cutganes

Hoabonomas

Rio Colorado

Del Norte

Alchedomas

Rio Salado

Rio Azul

S. Bartolome

S. Andres
Encarnacion

Casa Grande

Rio de Hila

S. Fernando

Vitoria

S. Dionisio
1700

YUMAS

S. Pedro

1699 COCO

Latinaja

M A R I C O P A S

S. Angelo

S. Catalina

S. Eugenio

S. Pantaleon

SOBA IPORIS

S. Pablo

Agua Escondida

Aguaje de la Luna

S. Mateo del
S. Felipe
Santiago

S. Simon

S. Tadeo

Del Baiqui

S. Bonifacio

S. Agustin

S. Cosme

Rosario

S. Marcos

S. Salvador

Bagiopas

Medanos
de Arena

Petaca

Carrizal

S. Francisco
S. Serafin

S. Francisco
Xauier del Bac

Quiburi

Quiquimas

Zojitos

Sero de
1698

S. Clara

La Merced

S. Rafael

S. Marcelo

La Merced

S. Cayetano
Reyes

Guebaui

S. Luis

S. Cruz

Sierra
Azul

S. Luis
del Bacapa

S. Eulalia

Busanic

S. Maria

S. Lazaro

Sierra Neuada

M A R   D E

Batequi
S. Eduardo
del Bagia

SOBAS

Tubutama

Sarie

Aquimuri

Himeres
Tupo

Remedios

Bacamichi

Bacuachi

Sierra del
Metcal

PARTE DE LA

Cocospora

Dolores

Chinape

S. Marcos

S. Mateo

Rio de S.
Ignacio

Nazarino

S. Ignacio

S. Madalena

Banami

R.ª
de S.
Iuan

Ochi

Guepaca

S. Iuan

Puerto de S. Sabina

Cucurpe

Tepoquis Tuape

Opodepe

Nacameri

SONORA

Acotzi

Babiacora

Matape

S. Rosalia
Insula

S. Agustin

NUEVA ESPAÑA

Populo

Angeles

Vres

S. Xauier

Alamos

S. Miguel

Tonichi

S. Antonio

SOBAS

PARTE DE LA CALIFORNIA

Insulas de Salsipuede

GUAIMAS

HIAQVI

Tecoripa

Nure

Onabas

Rio de S. Xauier

Rio de Sonora

Torin

Cocorin

Bican

Cedros

Comicari

Las Virgines

Tortuga

S. Ildefonso

Puerto de S. Xauier

Puerto de
S. Martin

Rio de Huiqui

MAYO

Guadalupe

Rio de S. Chriftoval

Bahia de la Concepcio

GUIMIES

Teboida
Reyes

S. Iuan

S. Bruno

Coronados

Rio de Mayo

Corrinpo
Hecabzoa
S. Cruz

R.ª de los
Frailes

B.ª de Ballen

S. Efteuan

S. Yfidro

Carmen

Bahia de
S. Lucas

Nabojae

Zibirijoa

MAR DEL ZUR

Bahia de las
Arenas

S.S. Inocentes

Santiago

Noche
Buena

S. Nicolas

Loreto

S. Xauier
Giganta

Farellon

Bahia de S. Mat

S. Miguel

Nachicahui
Chavri

Tegueco

Puerto de Ano Nueuo
defcubierto 1685

Rio de S. Tomas

EDUES

Puerto de Danzan
P.º de Matan

CINALOA

La Teta

A LA   C A L I F O R N I A

Traced 1948 by R. L. Ives

Father Kino not only explored much of Arizona but made accurate maps. This is a facsimile of his manuscript map of 1701 often pirated by publishers. It shows the "Passage by Land to California."

FOR A TIME the stalwart Jesuits worked alone in Pimeria Alta, "upper Pima country," and Father Kino was virtually the only missionary there until his death. Kino, a German-educated Italian born in 1645, spurned an academic career to join the Society of Jesus, and he arrived in New Spain in 1681. He was first assigned to a mission in Baja California, then sent into Sonora where he founded his own mission at Dolores. From 1691 to 1701 he established three missions within what is now Arizona: Tumacacori, Guevavi, and San Xavier del Bac. Although none of them became permanent towns, they were centers for acculturation of the Pima and Papago Indians.

Trained in astronomy and mathematics, Kino excelled as an explorer. At least six journeys were made to the Gila valley and twice he reached the Colorado, each time adding to the knowledge of the land as well as converting Indians who everywhere greeted the humble father with friendship.

After the Jesuits were expelled from New Spain in 1767, Pimeria Alta was turned over to the Franciscan Order. Father Francisco Hermenegildo Garces was assigned the mission of San Xavier del Bac. A worthy successor to Kino, Garces not only endeared himself to the Indians but explored the Gila Valley.

Kino's map of 1701, from an American woodcut of a German version. The Germans added the portion south of the dotted line and changed the date to 1702 (Hinton, 1878).

The church and plaza at Magdalena, Sonora, in 1864 (Browne, 1869). Kino died here in 1711, and historians assumed he was buried in this church. In 1966 Dr. William W. Wasley uncovered the foundation of another church under the plaza. Within it were the bones of Father Kino.

An artist's concept of Father Garcés at his campfire (James, 1906).

IN 1774 FATHER GARCES AND CAPTAIN DE ANZA led an expedition across the Sonoran Desert—not from Tubac where the soldiers were stationed but from Caborca in Sonora down the "Devil's Highway" to the site of modern Yuma, because that was the way Diaz had gone in 1540. Confirming the route from Yuma to San Gabriel, California, the soldier and priest returned via the Gila route to organize a major *entrada* to the Coast. In October 1775 they departed from Tubac with 240 people, soldiers and families, this time taking the easier way down the Santa Cruz River to the Gila and thence to the Yuma crossing. Garces and another Franciscan elected to stay among the seemingly friendly Yuma Indians, and Garces founded the Mission Purisimo de la Concepcion on the California side. During the year of American Independence, Father Garces, alone and afoot, trekked up the Colorado to The Needles, west to San Gabriel, back to the river and overland to the Hopi mesas. En route he descended into the Grand Canyon to visit the small tribe of Havasupai. At old Oraibi on the Fourth of July he dispatched a letter to the Franciscan mission at Zuni, then began to retrace his steps back to the Purisimo Mission. In September 1776 Garces was back at San Xavier after eleven months in the wilderness. In 1781 this remarkable man was killed by the Yuma.

Title page of the manuscript account kept by Father Pedro Font when he accompanied De Anza's *entrada* to California in 1775-76 (Bolton, 1933).

Ruins of the mission at Tumacacori, destroyed by the Apache (Gray, 1856).

The second Tumacacori mission as sketched by J. Ross Browne in 1863. The earlier Jesuit mission was razed by Apaches in 1776; this Franciscan church was started in the 1790s and abandoned in 1828 (Browne, 1864).

Padre Font's map of Arizona in 1777 (Bancroft, 1889).

The tiny church within the Tucson presidio, built in the 1780s. It apparently fell into disuse during the 1860s (*Prose & Poetry*, 1905).

Apache weapons and costumes (Brown, 1864).

The town of Tubac seen from the southeast with the Santa Rita Mountains in the background (Hinton, 1878).

FOLLOWING THE PIMA UPRISING of 1751, the governor of Sonora, Diego Ortiz de Parilla, was instructed to found a new presidio for fifty soldiers and their families in the northwest. He selected the site, the abandoned Pima village of Tubac. Its arrangement is shown in the contemporary map from the British Museum reproduced on the opposite page. In 1775 most of the garrison was sent to California to found another presidio to be called San Francisco, and next year the rest moved down the Santa Cruz 45 miles to the site of another Pima village called "San Agustin del Tucson." Despite Apache depredations, Tubac was occupied until the 1820s. Several German families en route to California settled here in the 1850s, and in 1856 Charles D. Poston moved the headquarters of his mining company into the old presidio.

The dilapidated presidio of Tubac in use by the Sonora Exploring and Mining Co. (Browne, 1869).

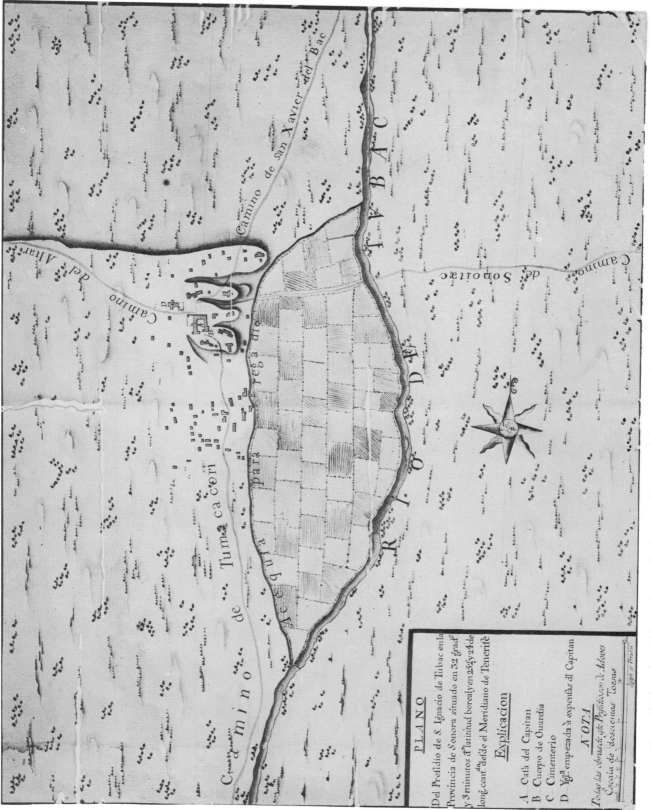

Plan of Tubac, first white settlement in Arizona, from an original map in the British Museum (courtesy of William A. Duffen, Tucson).

Engraving of San Xavier from a photograph
taken in the 1870s (Gleed, 1882).

THE WHITE DOVE OF THE DESERT: San
Xavier, the best example of a Spanish colo-
nial mission in the United States. After abandonment in 1828 it was rarely visited by the
clergy, but faithful Christian Indians would
not allow its destruction. Today it serves
Papago parishioners.

A distorted early lithograph
of San Xavier, useful
only to show details
(Parke, 1857).

J. Ross Browne's
accurate sketch
of San Xavier
(Browne, 1869).

THE HISTORY of Mission San Xavier del Bac epitomizes the ecclesiastical aspect of Hispanic Arizona. In 1700 the foundations of a church were begun at Bac—"a watering place in an otherwise dry river" as the Papagos called the ancient village site. The founder was Father Kino, the first of several priests who tended the mission until several German Jesuits took over. After the Pima Revolt the church decayed. In 1757 Father Alonso Espinosa constructed a new church, which was the home of the Franciscan Father Garces from 1768 to 1779. The third and present structure, the one so familiar to Southwestern travelers, was begun about 1783, a small distance south of the original Kino and Espinosa churches. It was started by Father Juan Bautista Velderrain, whose sister was married to the younger Juan Bautista de Anza (later governor of New Mexico). The third church stands to this day, whitewashed to gleam in the desert.

Facade of San Xavier del Bac
(Bishop, 1888).

Woodcut of the allegory of the Franciscans bringing civilization to Arizona, showing San Xavier in the center (Engelhardt, 1899).

For every mission like San Xavier that has been preserved, however, another has been abandoned or has lingered in impoverished decay. The chief difficulty in Pimeria Alta was the upsurge of Apache violence and plundering. In the 1760s they drove the Piman Sobaipuri out of the San Pedro Valley and in 1776 destroyed the Mission Tumacacori. By 1772, in fact, inspectors of New Spain's northwest frontier had concluded that the menace of non-mission Indians was greater than ever in all the provinces except California, and what few settlements had been made were on the verge of abandonment.

Interior of San Xavier, looking from the nave into the sanctuary (Bishop, 1888).

In 1772 King Carlos III published a new set of military regulations which authorized a single officer to supervise defense of the Interior Provinces (those on the frontier from California to Texas, including Sonora) and which prescribed a realignment of the presidios to be coupled with a vigorous war on the Comanche, Navajo, and Apache. This meant that the mission ceased to be the major instrument of civilization.

Lithograph of the Church of San Xavier, probably drawn from a photo (Hamilton, 1884).

An artist's imaginary concept of primitive hand-crushing of ore from early Spanish mines (*Harper's Monthly*, 1878).

The Salero ("salt cellar") mine, one of the few real mines found by Spaniards. Padres at Tumacacori are said to have made a salt cellar from solid silver from this mine (Browne, 1869).

THE FIRST COMMANDANT of the Interior Provinces of New Spain was, oddly enough, an Irishman —Colonel Hugo O'Conor, a mercenary long in the Spanish service. He was succeeded by a Frenchman, Brigadier Teodoro de Croix, whose uncle was Viceroy of New Spain. De Croix adjusted the cordon of frontier presidios, giving a free hand to such fighters as Colonel de Anza in New Mexico. Yet by 1785 the Apache were uncowed and had even broadened their scope of plunder. Then Bernardo de Galvez became viceroy with a plan which soon brought a tenuous peace to the frontier: prosecute the war at selected points; offer gifts to all who surrender; then supply the Apache with inferior firearms and all the booze they could drink. Within three years an uneasy peace spread over Sonora; the missions prospered; and many of the soldiers settled near presidios when their hitches were up.

A mule-powered *arrastra* for crushing ore (Hinton, 1878).

The hacienda of Babocomari near the later rail station of Fairbank and the San Pedro River. This stockraising grant extended 25 miles up Babocomari Creek and was established in 1832. Earlier, Father Kino had a *visita* (mission station) among the Sobaipuri Indians here (Gray, 1856).

Primitive Mexican plow
(Thayer, 1888) .

Burro loaded with wood
(Thayer, 1888) .

The Calabasas ranch which had a mission station in 1763 and was a thriving agricultural center on the Santa Cruz River throughout the Mexican period. Mount Wrightson is in the background (Gray, 1856).

The valley of Arivaca Creek with the Papago sacred mountain of Baboquivari jutting at left. Here was the Indian village of La Aribac with a mission station in 1733. In 1812 it was a stockraising grant and by 1856 was the headquarters of the Sonora Exploring and Mining Co. (Hinton, 1878).

The Spaniards brought wheat and ground it in crude flouring mills such as this (Thayer, 1888).

Mexican agriculture was primitive (Thayer, 1888).

Remington sketched an ox-powered cart (*Harper's*, 1890).

Solid-wheeled carts are still seen in northern Mexico (Thayer, 1888).

IN 1810 the oppressed people in Mexico rose in revolt, which continued until independence was won. In far-northern Pimeria Alta the War for Independence had little effect. In 1822 the commander of the presidio at Tucson simply took the oath of allegiance to the new government and went on fighting the Apache. By 1828 the cattle ranges, missions, and mines were abandoned.

Street scene of adobe Spanish residences (Conklin, 1878).

"A typical Mexican," according to a nineteenth-century writer. He may be overdrawn, but his sombrero, cigarette, and poncho passed into American culture long before the hippies (Wood, 1889).

An adobe corner fireplace, a distinctive feature of Mexican-style architecture (Thayer, 1888).

A Mexican *carreta*, almost the only form of wheeled transport in Sonora before the 1850s (Connelley, 1907).

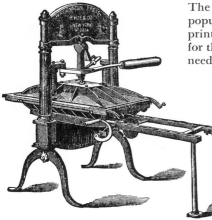

The Washington press was popular with frontier printers. It was adequate for the small pressruns needed (Ringwalt, 1871).

IN THE 1830s most of the rancheros took refuge in the walled town of Tucson, with the garrison at Tubac, or in fortified haciendas. The country had fewer white men by 1845 than in the previous century. Nearly the last act of the Mexican government in what shortly became Arizona was to attempt military colonization, in 1848. Meanwhile, the United States had provoked a war with Mexico and in 1846 the dusty columns of the gringo Army of the West marched down the Gila to conquer California. Eight years later President Santa Ana sold 29,640 square miles south of the Gila to the United States.

The first book printed in Arizona was a pastoral letter of the Bishop of Sonora. The press from which it emerged was a Washington hand-lever type carried to Tubac by the Santa Rita Silver Mining Company in the winter of 1858-59. The company published a newspaper, *The Weekly Arizonian*, that appeared for the first time in March of 1859, but in July the owners sold it to William S. Oury and Sylvester Mowry. The new owners moved the press to Tucson, employed J. Howard Wells as editor, and continued to publish the *Arizonian* until June of 1860. Sometime in August, 1859, or perhaps a bit later, Wells contracted with the Bishop of Sonora, Pedro Loza y Pardavé, to print a 20-page pamphlet written at Ures concerning the apostasy of a clergyman. It was titled "Pastoral Letter of the Bishop of Sonora, Don Pedro Loza, about a Personal Notice of the Priest Don Nieves Emigdio Acosta, Resident of Durango, Published in the Newspapers of Sonora and Sinaloa." Just why Bishop Loza took his printing to Tucson, in the United States, while there were presses in Sonora that he had previously hired, is not clear.

CARTA PASTORAL

DEL

OBISPO DE SONORA;

DN. PEDRO LOZA.

SOBRE UN REMITIDO

DEL

PBRO. DN. NIEVES EMIGDIO ACOSTA, DOMICILIARIO DE DURANGO, PUBLICADO EN LOS PERIÓDICOS **DE SONORA Y SINALOA.**

1859.

Caricature of the Bishop of Sonora (Cozzens, 1873).

Title page of the first book printed in Arizona, courtesy of the Pimeria Alta Historical Society, Nogales.

GUARANTEED CITIZENSHIP and property rights by the Gadsden Treaty, most of the Sonoranians in the Purchase stayed in what became Arizona and intermarried with Anglo settlers. Mexican-Americans have since contributed many traits of law, language, cuisine, and architecture to the state. Mining technology and the techniques of handling cattle from horseback were adopted from them as well.

The horses of northern Mexico were a favorite subject of Remington (*Outing*, 1887).

Home of L. C. Hughes, newspaper editor and territorial governor, at Court and Alameda streets in Tucson (Elliott, 1884).

IV. MAKING A TERRITORY

Two views of Guadalupe Canyon in southeastern Arizona (both from Bartlett, 1854). It was on Cooke's Wagon Road in 1846 and later was a point where travelers from Chihuahua joined the trail.

THE GADSDEN PURCHASE of 1853 foreshadowed a separate government for what is now Arizona. Without that area south of the Gila River, the unexplored wilderness to the north might have remained forever a part of New Mexico, which had been acquired in 1848 as a result of the Mexican War. Still, numerous Anglo-Americans had visited southern Arizona before 1853, and a score of mountain men had trapped beaver on the Salt, San Francisco, San Pedro, Gila, Verde, and Colorado rivers.

Sugar Loaf Mountain (El Peloncillo), a landmark on the Tucson cutoff from Cooke's Road (Hinton, 1878).

Apaches watching a wagon train (Dunn, 1886).

THE GOLD RUSH OF '49 turned attention to southern trails such as Cooke's Wagon Road that had been trod by the Mormon Battalion from the Rio Grande to Guadalupe Pass and on through Sonora to Tucson. Emigrants soon cut off many miles by striking due west from about modern Lordsburg, New Mexico, to Apache Pass, thence to Tucson.

Apache Pass in the Chiricahua Range. Cannon and parapet were added by the artist to represent Fort Bowie built in 1862 (Bell, 1870).

Santa Cruz was the most important town in Sonora on the Gila Trail. J. Ross Browne sketched the church there in 1864 (Browne, 1869).

VERY POPULAR WAS the trail from Franklin, Texas (now El Paso), or from the Mexican east coast into Chihuahua, thence to a junction with Cooke's Road in Guadalupe Canyon. All of these southern trails were loosely called "the Gila Trail" because they converged on the Gila River at the Pima Villages before going to California.

The valley leading north to Tucson from Santa Cruz was pictured by H. C. Pratt (Bartlett, 1854).

Bartlett sketched Santa Cruz, above, in 1852 (Bartlett, 1854).

Tucson, Sonora, in 1852. The lithograph was made from a watercolor sketch by J. R. Bartlett. The artist is seen shaded by an umbrella on the east slope of Sentinel Peak. The buildings in the foreground are a Franciscan mission school and beyond the town is the Santa Catalina range (Bartlett, 1854).

HOWEVER THEY CAME, travelers eventually reached the presidial town of Tucson. Until 1856, it was protected by a few *soldados de cuera* under Captain Antonio Comaduran and was supplied by rancheros in the Santa Cruz valley. After a little rest in Tucson, California-bound emigrants made a beeline across the desert toward El Picacho, a 3,400-foot volcanic plug midway to the Pima villages.

El Picacho from the north (Browne, 1869).

An emigrant camp on the Gila Trail (James, 1906).

El Picacho seen from the south. As the name means "the peak," reference to "Picacho Peak" is redundant. A Civil War skirmish was fought here in April, 1862, when Confederate soldiers ambushed the advance guard of the California Column. Later the Southern Pacific laid tracks over the Union soldiers' graves. (Bartlett, 1854).

The irrigated fields of the Pima (below), viewed from Sacaton Butte (Bartlett, 1854). The Gila River Indian Reservation south of modern Phoenix includes this fertile valley where wheat, melons, and fruit are still raised for sale.

The flood plain of the Gila (Bartlett, 1854).

STOCK and abundant food supplies could be obtained from the friendly Pima and Maricopa. From their villages it was 40 miles across the desert to the Great Bend of the Gila and another 130 along the stream to Fort Yuma. The river provided plenty of drinking water but it was generally too shallow to carry boats, though a few emigrants tried. The first year of the Gold Rush must have been very wet, for in November a family named Howard took a sixteen-foot flatboat all the way to the mouth from the Pima villages. En route Mrs. Howard gave birth to a son appropriately named Gila.

Oatman Flat, a little below modern Gila Bend, where the Oatman family was massacred. The mountains in the distance are the Gila Bend range north of the river (Browne, 1869).

LEAVING THE GILA with full water casks, emigrants skirted the Sierra Estrella to the south and struck due west toward a low pass in the Maricopa Mountains to descend again into the Gila valley where the river resumes a westward course. The road for much of the way followed the north side of the stream.

Antelope Hill. J. Ross Browne exaggerated the landmark in this sketch; actually the volcanic outcrop rises no more than 500 feet from the south bank of the Gila. There was a stagecoach and government forage station here in the 1860s (Browne, 1869).

Mission Camp on the Gila about fifteen miles below Antelope Hill. Coronation Peak rises north of the river (Browne, 1869).

SIXTY MILES FROM Oatman Flat, after three days or more of travel, emigrants came in sight of Antelope Hill, and fifteen miles below was Mission Camp. Now on the south side, they would come at last to the Colorado River opposite Fort Yuma in California. It was nearly 700 miles from Fort Bliss, Texas.

A romantic view of the Gila River in flood, at the point where it joins the Colorado several miles above Fort Yuma (Bartlett, 1854).

Lieutenant William H. Emory's camp at the junction of the Gila and Colorado rivers in November, 1846. Emory's account of his trip with General Kearny became the basis for emigrant guides for the southern route to California (Emory, 1848).

Camp Yuma, California, overlooked the Colorado River crossing from Arizona. It was first occupied in 1849 and was permanently established in 1851. This picture, drawn in December, 1851, is the earliest known (Sitgreaves, 1854).

THE FIRST ANGLOS into Arizona were the fur trappers who ventured west from the Rio Grande. James Ohio Pattie may have been first, in 1824, followed by Ewing Young, William Sherley Williams, and Antoine Leroux.

"Mr. Pattie wounded by an Indian arrow," perhaps the first picture of an Arizona scene, from *The Personal Narrative of James O. Pattie of Kentucky* (Flint, 1831).

"Kit" Carson was a young trapper with Ewing Young in Arizona (Frost, 1850).

A "mountain man" of the Old West, by Remington (*Harper's Monthly*, 1891).

"The Fate of Bill Williams," shot by Ute Indians in a Colorado snowstorm, as imagined by an artist (Brewerton, 1853).

William H. Emory was a topographical engineer with Kearny and later ran a boundary line with Mexico (*Appleton's*, 1889).

John Mix Stanley's picture of Emory meeting the Pima and Coco-Maricopa Indians in 1846 (Emory, 1848).

Brigadier General Philip St. George Cooke led the Mormon Battalion through Arizona during the Mexican War (*Century*, 1887).

Major General Stephen Watts Kearny
(Frost, 1850).

John C. Frémont's stormy career touched Arizona twice. After an ill-fated winter expedition that left him recovering in Taos, New Mexico, he organized an expedition over the Gila Trail in February, 1849. In 1878 he was appointed governor of Arizona Territory (*Century*, 1887).

THE MEXICAN WAR and the subsequent Gold Rush brought Americans in large numbers to Arizona, although most of them only passed through. As soon as New Mexico was in American hands, Kearny led 300 dragoons down the Gila valley and went on to seize Alta California. The Treaty of Guadalupe Hidalgo that concluded the war did not transfer the settled part of Arizona south of the Gila.

Map showing the boundary set by the Treaty of Guadalupe Hidalgo (Mansfield, 1848).

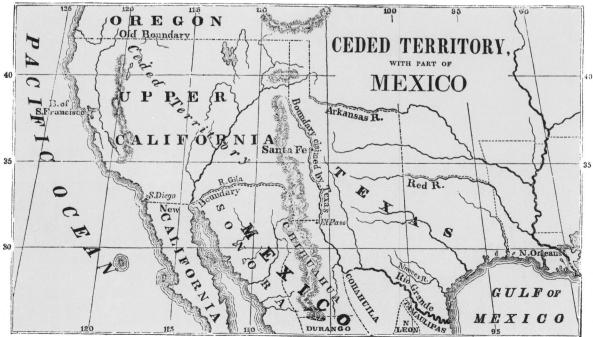

As NEWS SPREAD that gold had been discovered on the American River in California in January 1848, frenzied argonauts rushed to seek their fortune. Between 1848 and 1853 perhaps 60,000 reached Fort Yuma en route over the Gila Trail or over the Camino del Diablo. A proposed railroad to be built along the Gila and the dispute over the boundary as described in the treaty ending the war were primary motives for a new treaty. Thus James Gadsden agreed to pay Mexico $10 million for concession of the Mesilla Valley and a strip south of the Gila. Nearly thirty years were to pass before any railroad crossed Arizona, but emigrants kept coming and a backwash of disappointed gold seekers even returned to settle the Gadsden Strip.

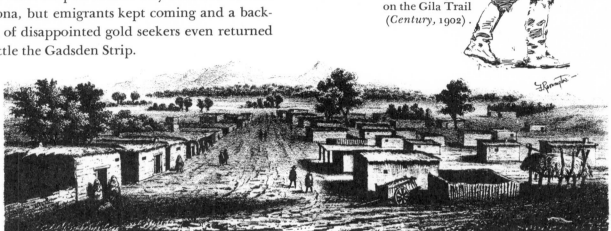

A Texan emigrant on the Gila Trail (*Century, 1902*).

Mesilla, New Mexico, almost became capital of Arizona (Gray, 1856).

Cochise looks like a stock Indian in this woodcut of his purported 1859 meeting with S. W. Cozzens (Cozzens, 1873).

After the cession of New Mexico in 1848, dissatisfied Mexicans on the upper Rio Grande moved south into the Mesilla Valley, assumed to be in Chihuahua. The region's ownership, however, was disputed and in 1853 Santa Ana conceded a 31° 47′ line when Gadsden purchased a strip of territory west to the Colorado. The entire area was soon called Arizona in which the town of Mesilla was the largest with over 2,000 citizens. If an east-west line had been drawn across New Mexico to create the later territory, the town would have been its capital.

Massacre of the Oatman family.

NO TRAVELERS on the Gila Trail were so well known as the Oatman family. Their harrowing tale was read in 26,000 copies of a book first published in 1857. The Oatmans—husband, wife, and seven children—moved with about fifty other emigrants from Missouri in the autumn of 1850. Some rested at Tucson but most pushed on to the Pima Villages. In February, 1851, Royse Oatman decided to go it alone to California. On the 18th they were attacked by Yavapai just beyond the Great Bend of the Gila. (All pictures on this page from Stratton, 1858.)

Olive and Mary in the Yavapai Indian Camp.

Lorenzo Oatman in later years (left) and at the massacre scene (right).

THE SAVAGES CARRIED off Olive, aged sixteen, and Mary Ann, ten, leaving the others for dead. Lorenzo, Olive's fourteen-year-old brother, was only stunned. He got back to Maricopa Wells and traveled with the other emigrants to Fort Yuma where he told his horrible story to Major Samuel P. Heintzelman. The girls were sold as slaves to the Mojave who treated them relatively well, but Mary Ann died of starvation. In 1857 Olive was purchased by white men from Fort Yuma and reunited with her brother who had never ceased his efforts to find her. After attending college, she married J. B. Fairchild of New York. They removed to Sherman, Texas, where she died in 1903.

Olive Oatman, after her rescue, still bore Mojave tattooing. (Stratton, 1858).

Olive Oatman before the Indian council which decided to adopt her (Stratton, 1858).

John Russell Bartlett was an eminent scholar, librarian, and artist who was appointed as U.S.-Mexican boundary commissioner in 1850. He was a poor judge of men and ignorant of geodesy. Although his efforts failed to establish a boundary, his two-volume narrative of travel is a Southwestern classic (*Appleton's*, 1889).

AMERICAN TROOPS OCCUPIED the Mesilla Valley in 1851, but it was five years before dragoons marched to Tucson. In 1857 they built Fort Buchanan on Sonoita Creek. Yet before the U.S. Congress had approved Gadsden's treaty, Charles D. Poston with associates from San Francisco had investigated the mines of Arizona and by 1856 a Cincinnati syndicate incorporated the Sonora Exploring and Mining Company for $1 million.

The map below shows the boundary dispute, with varying claims. Bartlett's survey claimed the line A-B-C. The Mexicans claimed line D-E-F. The inaccurate Disturnell map, mentioned in the initial treaty, showed line A-H-I. The Gadsden Treaty finally specified the line A-H-J-K (Bancroft, 1889).

Richard S. Ewell, "Old Baldy." As a captain of dragoons he commanded Fort Buchanan and also mined for silver. Enthusiastic Arizonans named a county for him in 1860 (Moat, 1896).

Samuel P. Heintzelman commanded Fort Yuma as a major of infantry. He was also president of the Sonora Exploring and Mining Co. (*Appleton's*, 1889).

One of the boundary monuments near modern Nogales, erected by Major Emory in 1855 (Browne, 1869).

Charles D. Poston joined with Samuel Heintzelman in forming a mining company at Tubac (Browne, 1869).

THE SONORA EXPLORING AND MINING CO., headed by Heintzelman and Poston, took up quarters at the abandoned presidio of Tubac. Other entrepreneurs and merchants moved to Tucson, Mesilla, and near new military posts. Stockmen reoccupied abandoned ranches. The rancho of Arivaca was the center of operations for the Sonora Company's best producer, the Cerro Colorado Silver mine renamed the Heintzelman. A subsidiary company, formed to work claims in the Santa Rita Mountains, imported a press and started a newspaper.

Masthead of Arizona's first newspaper, 1859.

Edward E. Cross edited Arizona's first newspaper. He died at Gettysburg (*Century*, 1886).

THE WEEKLY ARIZONIAN.

VOL. 1. TUBAC, ARIZONA MARCH 3, 1859. No. 1.

THE ARIZONIAN,
A WEEKLY PAPER,

DEVOTED TO THE GENERAL INTERESTS OF ARIZONA.

—TERMS:—

Single copies, per annum, - - $3 00

RATES OF ADVERTISING:

One Square, of 10 lines, or less, one insertion, $2 00
"   "   "   "   three   4 00
"   "   "   "   one quarter,   10 00
"   "   "   "   one year,   30 00

All communications and business letters must be addressed to THE ARIZONIAN, Tubac, Arizona.

Mexican Politics.

There are in Mexico three great leading parties, answering to the type of party wherever that product of imperfect civilization exists. The first, because the eldest, is the CONSERVATIVE, with principles cognate with its name; strenuously adhering to ancient realism as distinguished from modern speculation; anxious to concentrate power in individual hands, and therefore to weaken the authority of popular constitutions and popular legislation; dependent upon the sympathy of the Church and the onfort who only abandoned power to place all its resources at the command of the enemies of popular rights; and, to whose weakness more than to any other cause, Mexico is this day indebted for the lamentable confusion into which its affairs have fallen. If the events of the past year have proved anything, it is that the Liberal cause is predominant everywhere outside of the capital; and that the Constitution which Comonfort betrayed met, in a general sense, the wants and wishes of the people. The only point unattainable to the popular party is the City of Mexico, which it was in the power of Comonfort to have secured to them. He gave it to their adversaries, and hence this protracted series of woes.

Since the departure of Comonfort to the United States, there has been a constant state of warfare between the opposing factions, with varied success, until very lately, when the Conservatives are reported to have triumphed, and elected General Miramon President. We may, however, still look for a continuance of this strife between the various parties.

Condition of Mexico.

The London Times uses strong language in its articles on Mexico. In an article written

Leech's Wagon Road.

Before Congress grants further appropriations for "wagon roads," we venture the suggestion that some official investigation be instituted as to the expenditures made and the work done by late expeditions. If no more good was accomplished by the northern wagon road companies than was effected by Colonel Leech and his corps on the Southern line, the money might as well be kept in the Treasury.

From El Paso, along the old road to Tucson, to the point where Leech's road strikes off to the Gila, the amount of labor performed was very trifling. As to the road along the Gila, we doubt very much if it has ever been traveled by a wagon since the expedition left, and the faint tracks made by the expedition wagons are rapidly growing up to grass. Col. Leech's ox train, under the superintendence of a sea captain, was eleven months making the distance from Fort Belknap to La Mesilla and arrived just in time to be sold out, not having been of the least benefit. There are circumstances getic individuals may have made "four" dollars per day, which is a very fine average yield of the diggings, but the "hundred-and-fifty-dollars-per-day"-men it would puzzle even a "Washington correspondent" to discover.

We are next enlightened to the effect that:

A new silver "lead" had been discovered on land belonging to Lieut. Mowry, which pays as richly as, if not richer, than the celebrated Heintzelman silver mine. These more recent discoveries had produced an excited mining fever throughout the country.

In view of the fact that silver mining is receiving considerable attention in this section of Arizona, we should really be glad to know by whom that identical "lead" (on land belonging to Lieut Mowry,) was discovered, when, and where? We feel confident that such' information will be "new" to our readers, and no doubt highly gratifying. We shall also be equally gratified if the New York Times will designate some particular locality in this Territory where a few cases of the above mentioned "mining fever" may be found!

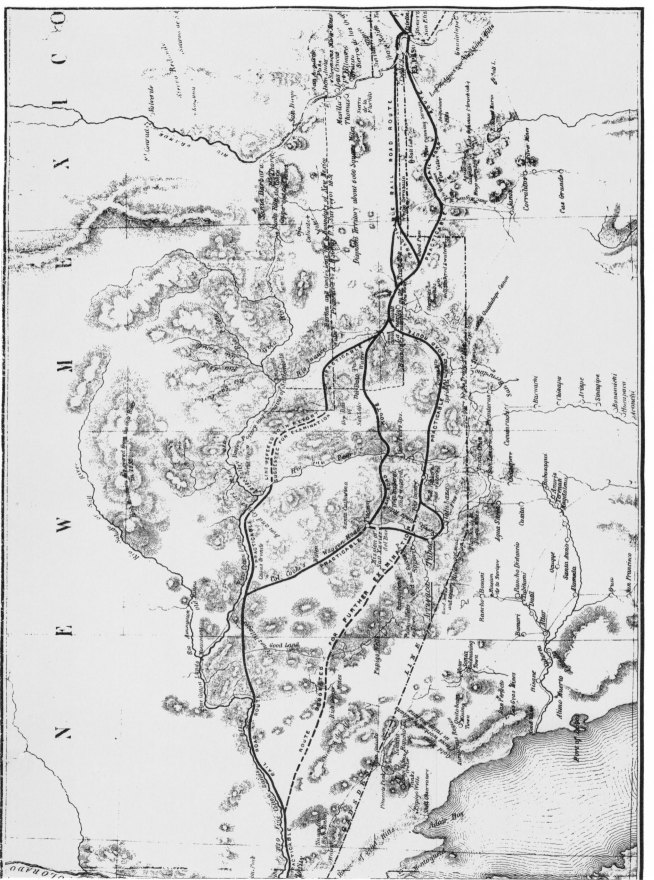

"Map of Proposed Arizona Territory" that accompanied Sylvester Mowry's *Memoir* in 1857.

THE CUTTING EDGE of serious exploration in Arizona was the army's elite Corps of Topographical Engineers, who mapped the land, made scientific examinations, and established routes that thousands followed.

Amiel Weeks Whipple, a topographical engineer, explored northern Arizona in 1853-1854. He was killed in the Civil War (*Century*, 1886).

Francois X. Aubry, famed horseman, drove a band of sheep from the Rio Grande to California in 1852 and later found gold on the Colorado. In 1854 he returned from a similar trip along the 35th Parallel route that had just been explored by A. W. Whipple (Twitchell, 1912).

Whipple's men resting in Lithodendron Wash, now in the Petrified Forest (Whipple, 1856).

State Highway 68 now runs through Union Pass, located in 1851 by Lorenzo Sitgreaves while seeking an easy grade through the Black Mountains (Sitgreaves, 1854).

Edward Fitzgerald Beale, a naval officer who joined the Army of the West in the Mexican War, had an encounter with Indians while riding through Arizona with dispatches (Frost, 1850).

A typical explorers' camp. This lithograph, after Möllhausen, shows Lt. Whipple's camp at the southern end of the Aquarius Mountains in January, 1854 (Whipple, 1856).

Whipple's exploring party in the valley of the Bill Williams River, 1854, from a sketch by Lieutenant John C. Tidball. This stream is known as the Santa Maria above its junction with the Big Sandy River, and Whipple traversed its full length in search of a railroad passage (Whipple, 1856).

Whipple's party crossing the Colorado River near the Mojave Indian villages, February 27, 1854. Lithograph on stone by J. J. Young after a sketch by Möllhausen (Whipple, 1856).

THE PRINCIPAL GOVERNMENT EXPEDITIONS into Arizona were conducted by Amiel W. Whipple, Edward F. Beale, and Joseph C. Ives. Whipple started at Fort Smith, Arkansas, and made a reconnaissance west along the 35th Parallel to beyond the Colorado River in 1853-54. His work included an exhaustive scientific study as well as a topographic survey. Beale was a former Navy lieutenant who developed a passion for camels as transportation on Western deserts. He induced Secretary of War Jefferson Davis to buy several score dromedaries and Bactrian camels in North Africa, and in 1857 Beale got his chance to prove his theories. He opened a wagon road through Arizona from Zuni to the Colorado, but the beasts were more of a nuisance than mules and the experiment was abandoned. Joseph Christmas Ives explored the Colorado River, starting by steamboat from Fort Yuma in January, 1858. He mapped the river as far as Black Canyon, then he sent the boat back and marched overland to Fort Defiance. He was the first Anglo to descend into the Grand Canyon.

Edward Fitzgerald Beale in his camel driver's costume (courtesy Arizona Pioneers' Historical Society).

A camel train in Nevada. When the army disbanded its camel corps, it sold the animals to miners and freighters. A few more were also imported by civilians and were used in Nevada (Clampitt, 1888).

Dr. John S. Newberry accompanied the Ives expedition as geologist (*Appleton's*, 1889).

Ives' steamboat, *Explorer,* at Deep Rapid, now Lake Mojave behind Davis Dam (Ives, 1861).

Top of the *Explorer*'s stack shows above the bank as the boat gets up steam. In the distance are the Purple Hills (Ives, 1861).

The steamboat *Explorer* as lithographed by J. J. Young from a sketch by Möllhausen. The mountain in the background is Chimney Peak. The boat, 54 feet long and made of iron, was built in Philadelphia, tested on the Delaware River, then broken down and carried to the mouth of the Colorado to be reassembled (Ives, 1861).

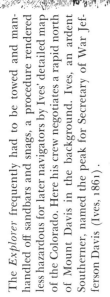

The *Explorer* frequently had to be towed and man-handled off sandbars and snags, a procedure rendered less hazardous for later navigators by Ives' detailed map of the Colorado. Here his crew negotiates a rapid north of Mount Davis in the background. Ives, an ardent Southerner, named the peak for Secretary of War Jefferson Davis (Ives, 1861).

The *Explorer* in Black Canyon, a gorge on the river nearly twenty miles long with walls of dark rhyolite. Ives concluded that a point halfway through this gorge was the practical head of navigation, but steamers later regularly visited Callville, Nevada, nearly twenty miles farther north (Möll-hausen, 1861).

The camp of Ives' exploring party north of present-day Flagstaff in 1858. The *Explorer* had been sent with a crew back to Fort Yuma while Ives marched overland to Fort Defiance with Dr. Newberry and an escort of 20 soldiers. They were caught by a late snow, a surprisingly common occurrence in a land usually thought of as a desert. This lithograph by J. J. Young is after a sketch by Möllhausen (Ives, 1861).

JOHN GRUBB PARKE, then a lieutenant with the U.S. Topographical Engineers and later a general, in 1854-55 surveyed the proposed route for a railroad through Arizona, from San Diego to the Rio Grande. The party of Andrew B. Gray was also in the field for the Texas Western Railroad Company and met Parke in the Sulphur Springs Valley. Parke surveyed two routes from the Pima villages to the Rio Grande, one by way of Tucson and the other via the San Pedro valley. He recommended the latter.

John Grubb Parke
(*Appleton's*, 1889).

Parke's camp at Maricopa Wells, where a permanent supply of good water was found, about seven miles north of modern Maricopa. The Sierra Estrella is in the background (Parke, 1857).

"A Rush for New Diggings" by H. C. Redwood illustrates a phase of Gold Rush history not only in California but all through the West. Many such prospectors—and the merchants, gamblers, and whiskey peddlers who followed them—crossed the Colorado to search for gold (*Century*, 1891).

BY THE EVE of the Civil War, Arizona had been mapped, its principal roads laid out, and the Army had established posts. The Census of 1860 showed over 4,000 people living in the southern part of New Mexico set aside as the "County of Arizona" which was already seeking territorial status.

Railroad surveyors making a reconnaissance for the Kansas Pacific Railway in southeastern Arizona (Bell, 1870).

William Sanders Oury, rancher, politician, and Indian fighter (courtesy William A. Duffen).

SOME NOTABLE TERRITORIAL promoters were William Oury, Charles Poston, and C. P. Stone. Oury served in Texas' fight for independence and followed the Gold Rush to California before settling south of Tucson. He and his brother Granville urged Arizonans to join the Confederacy. Poston managed the Sonora Company's properties around Tubac but fled the Apache-infested country in 1861. Captain Stone left the army to make land surveys for a Mexican banking firm, later obtained a federal road building contract in Arizona. He reentered the army when the Civil War began and became a general.

Charles DeBrille Poston left the study of law in Kentucky to seek his fortune in California. Although his mining efforts in Arizona collapsed, he was briefly rewarded for his work to gain territorial status by election to Congress. The rest of his life was spent in minor government jobs (Poston, 1878).

Charles Pomeroy Stone, surveyor and road builder who established Camp Jecker near the Patagonia Mine and later built the El Paso-Fort Yuma road (*Appleton's*, 1889).

The Cerro Colorado silver mine near Arivaca, later renamed the Heintzelman Mine (Browne, 1869).

Colt's company store at Tubac energetically pushed the latest fruits of his inventive genius, a line of revoving cylinder rifles. Below left is the "sporting rifle" and right is the "military carbine," both of which occasionally spewed the shooter's face with burning powder. Relatively few of these weapons were produced and perhaps a majority were sold in Arizona where every man went armed (courtesy James E. Serven).

Samuel Colt took over the Sonora Exploring and Mining Co. when its organizers failed either to meet obligations or to amass enough capital to develop their mineral claims. Colt reorganized the company in New York in 1859, then sent a new agent to Arizona to replace Poston (courtesy James E. Serven).

The mill, reduction plant, and living quarters of the Santa Rita silver mines, 15 miles east of Tubac in early 1864. These mines, a subsidiary of the Sonora Exploring and Mining Co., were abandoned when the war broke out. In the background are the Grosvenor Hills seen on p. 40 (Browne, 1869).

FOREMOST OF THE petitioners for territorial government were Major S. P. Heintzelman and Sylvester Mowry. Mowry, a miner and land speculator, was an articulate lobbyist before the Civil War but lost favor because of his pro-slavery views. Heintzelman, onetime president of the Sonora Company, became a general when the war began and soon found himself in Washington where he was joined by Charles Poston. They were not slow to use their influence with Congress and the President.

Advocates of territorial status were primarily interested in federal protection of their enterprises. Congress had little sympathy and sectional quarrels precluded passage of an organic act in the 1850s. Yet the war was to provide a catalyst for action. In the spring of 1862 a thrust by Texan invaders planted a Confederate territorial government at Mesilla. In the next few months loyal forces in California and Colorado moved to liberate New Mexico, and Congress prudently organized a Union territory to keep the inhabitants loyal. On February 24, 1863, Abraham Lincoln signed the act to create Arizona, dividing New Mexico on the 109th Meridian. John Noble Goodwin was selected to be governor. Arriving in the territory in December, Goodwin designated Fort Whipple in Chino Valley as a capital. But gold had been found on the headwaters of the Hassayampa, and in the spring of 1864 the governor took the capital as well as the fort to Granite Creek where the city of Prescott arose.

Grave of an Apache victim on the Santa Cruz road (Browne, 1869).

Smelter of the Mowry silver mine (Browne, 1869).

Sylvester Mowry, an ex-lieutenant of artillery, purchased an Arizona silver mine in 1860 and was making money when the Civil War broke out. He was arrested by General Carleton as a Southern sympathizer in 1862 and his mine was confiscated (Browne, 1869).

Primitive methods of mining are evident in this sketch of the Mowry Mine, first discovered in 1857 and then named the "Patagonia." During the Civil War capital and machinery were scarce. Peons removed ore and transported it in native carts to the nearby hacienda (Browne, 1869).

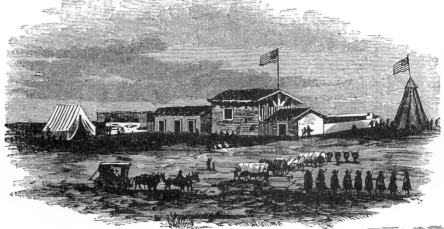

Grist mill and home of Ammi M. White near the Pima villages where he obtained his grain. Sometimes called the Casa Blanca, White's Mill was on the south side of the Gila, west of present Florence. White married a Maricopa woman, was captured by the Confederates in 1862, and later served as Indian agent to the Pimas (Browne, 1869).

Ruins of William B. Rhodes' ranch in the Santa Cruz valley, near the modern Canoa Ranch. Rhodes is best known for his daring fight with Apaches and the hairbreadth escape which Raphael Pumpelly immortalized in a book (Browne, 1869).

During the Confederate invasion of New Mexico, 200 mounted Texans under Captain Sherod Hunter rode over to occupy Tucson. Some of them probably looked like the "ranger" above (Lossing, 1877).

When J. Ross Browne came through Tucson in 1864 he found the soldiers primarily engaged in drinking and gambling, which inspired his cartoon, "Rear View of Tucson." During the Civil War the California Column liberated Arizona from the Confederates, fought a skirmish at Picacho Pass, and had a real battle with Apache for possession of Apache Pass. Numerous military camps were established; the one at Tucson became a permanent post as Fort Lowell (Browne, 1869).

John Noble Goodwin, first territorial governor of Arizona (*Frank Leslie's*, 1863).

First seal of the territorial government (Bancroft, 1889).

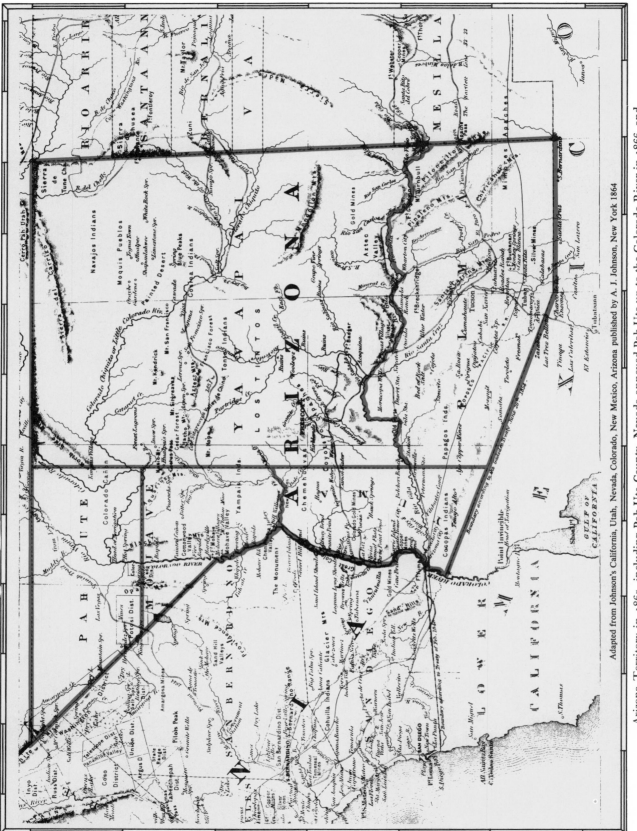

Arizona Territory in 1865, including Pah-Ute County. Nevada annexed Pah-Ute up to the Colorado River in 1866, and the gambling resort of Las Vegas is located in Arizona's "lost county."

Adapted from Johnson's California, Utah, Nevada, Colorado, New Mexico, Arizona published by A. J. Johnson, New York 1864

V. APACHE WARS

Apache captive crucified by the Maricopa (Browne, 1869).

The frequent fate of a lone white man in the 1880s was sketched by Remington for Lieutenant Bigelow's account of the Apache wars (*Outing*, 1887).

NOTHING WAS POSSIBLE in Arizona until the Apache problem was solved. A bloody vendetta, inherited from Mexican conquest, had been abetted by scalp hunters in the 1830s and 1840s. The Pima and Maricopa also warred on the Apache, their traditional foe. Miners around Prescott compounded the problem by wantonly killing other Indians. General Carleton's policy of extermination, officially unapproved, was continued by civilians after 1863.

James H. Carleton, who had led the California Column across Arizona, assumed the wartime governorship of New Mexico in 1862. He began a policy of extermination continued, after Arizona became a territory, by civilians and assisted by volunteer soldiers.

Apaches usually ambushed small parties, such as this attack on the heavily armed escort of
Samuel F. Butterworth, president of the Arizona Mining Co., in 1863 (Browne, 1869).

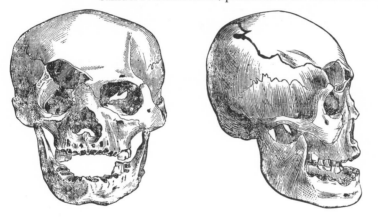

No authentic pictures are known of Cochise and
Mangas Colorado, the greatest Apache leaders,
but the bullet-punctured skull of the giant Mangas was preserved (Beadle, 1873). The Chiricahua chief was captured by soldiers in 1862 and
shot "trying to escape." A soldier scalped him
and his skull was sent to the Smithsonian Institution.

Captain R. S. Ewell commanded Fort Buchanan in
1860 (*Appleton's*, 1889).

Ewell led his dragoons in several successful
pursuits of marauding Apache (Cozzens,
1873).

Christopher "Kit" Carson, onetime trapper and mountain man, was a brigadier general who, in 1863, induced the Navajo to surrender (*Century*, 1891).

J. Ross Browne drew this cartoon of an "Arizonian in sight of home" to emphasize desolation by Apache (Browne, 1869).

Some Tucson citizens and Papago Indians, led by William Oury, massacred over a hundred Aravaipa Apache near Camp Grant in 1871. Oury claimed the Apache were raiding ranches in the Santa Cruz valley while accepting rations from the army.

APACHE DEPREDATIONS caused whites to kill indiscriminately, which in turn brought Apache vengeance down on the whites. In 1867 the regular army arrived to furnish protection. Under General George Stoneman, efforts were made to settle the less hostile bands around the army posts ("feeding stations," the civilians derisively called them), but he did not seem willing or able to punish the wild bands.

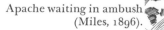

Apache waiting in ambush (Miles, 1896).

George Stoneman was first commander of the Arizona department. He had been a dashing cavalry leader in the Civil War. In 1871 he was replaced by George Crook. Both men disliked Arizona Indian war profiteers (*Appleton's,* 1889).

Fort Whipple near Prescott was always headquarters of the Military Department of Arizona, although far removed from the last campaigns of the 1880s. It was a crude log post in the 1860s, one of the few in the Southwest with a palisade. In the 1870s it was moved to higher ground and rebuilt of more substantial material. Today it is a U.S. Veterans' hospital (Campion, 1878).

Fort Defiance, technically the first military post in Arizona, was founded in 1851 near Canyon de Chelly. New Mexico's border then included Fort Defiance, which was abandoned in 1861. It was reoccupied briefly by General Carson's troops in 1863-1864 and became the Navajo Indian Agency four years later. It was always administered from Santa Fe and never considered part of the Arizona department although it now lies within Arizona (Davis, 1857).

An officer in the
uniform of the 1850s
(*Century*, 1902).

Fort Bowie was established by the California volunteers in 1862 at the "Puerto del Dado"
in the Apache Pass at the north end of the Chiricahua Mountains. Permanent water made
the pass useful for emigrants and the Overland Mail (*Wonderful Adventures*, 1874).

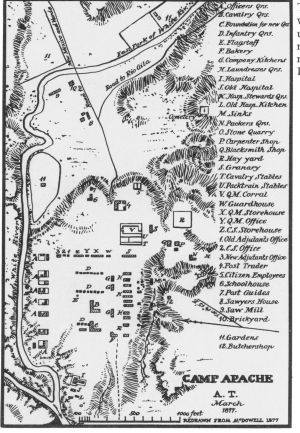

A. Officers Qrs.
B. Cavalry Qrs.
C. Foundation for new Qrs.
D. Infantry Qrs.
E. Flagstaff
F. Bakery
G. Company Kitchens
H. Laundresses Qrs.
I. Hospital
J. Old Hospital
K. Hosp. Stewards Qrs.
L. Old Hosp. Kitchen
M. Sinks
N. Packers Qrs.
O. Stone Quarry
P. Carpenter Shop
Q. Blacksmith Shop
R. Hay yard
S. Granary
T. Cavalry Stables
U. Packtrain Stables
V. Q.M. Corral
W. Guardhouse
X. Q.M. Storehouse
Y. Q.M. Office
Z. C.S. Storehouse
1. Old Adjutants Office
2. C.S. Office
3. New Adjutants Office
4. Post Trader
5. Citizen Employees
6. Schoolhouse
7. Post Guides
8. Sawyers House
9. Saw Mill
10. Brickyard

11. Gardens
12. Butchershop

CAMP APACHE

A. T.
March
1877.
REDRAWN FROM McDOWELL 1877

The plan of Camp Apache is typical of Southwestern army posts. Founded in 1870, it was
used by Crook in 1872-1873 and survives as a
reservation school (From McDowell, 1877;
redrawn by Brandes; courtesy Dale Stuart
King, publisher).

Camp McDowell on the Salt River was built in
1865 by California troops (Hinton, 1878).

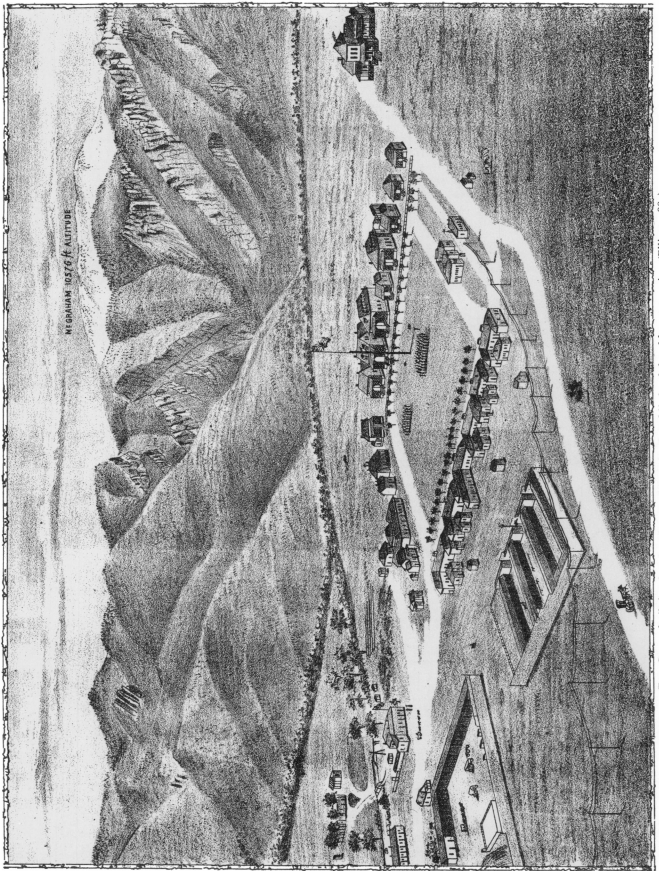

MT GRAHAM 10,517 ft ALTITUDE

Fort Grant, built in 1872, is today a reform school and little of the old post remains (Elliott, 1884).

The arrival of Olive Oatman at Fort Yuma after her rescue from the Mojave Indians in 1857 (Stratton, 1858).

Samuel P. Heintzelman as a major general in the Civil War. He began the permanent fort at Yuma in 1851 and here met Charles Poston on the way to investigate mines in the Gadsden Strip (*Century*, 1884).

FORT GRANT, shown on the opposite page, was established in 1872, twenty-seven miles north of Willcox. It was one of the largest, most solidly built posts in Arizona and was occupied until 1908. Nearby was the "hog ranch" called Bonita, where soldiers and desperadoes rubbed elbows; Billy, the Kid, killed a man there. A few miles west was H. C. Hooker's Sierra Bonita Ranch; his daughter married a 7th Cavalry officer at the fort. There was an earlier post named for General Grant on the San Pedro River near Aravaipa Canyon.

A panorama of the Yuma Crossing of the Colorado, showing Fort Yuma in California on the far bank (Bartlett, 1854).

The attack led by Lieutenant William J. Ross, 23rd Infantry, at dawn of December 28, 1872, on an Apache camp in the Salt River Canyon. This opened the Battle of the Caves, one of Crook's most successful engagements. Most of seventy-five hostiles were killed (*Century*, 1891).

GEORGE CROOK, lieutenant colonel of the 23rd Infantry, came to Arizona from Oregon in June 1871 and took command on his brevet rank of major general. After a reconnaissance of the Chiricahua country, he went to Camp Apache in the White Mountains and induced a few Coyotero Apache to enlist in the army as scouts. Enthusiastic reports of their conduct convinced Crook to make them an essential part of his plans. A second element in his thinking was the employment of mule packtrains; a thousand were organized into trains of fifty each, to accompany every column of troops that took the field.

Mike Burns, an eight year old Apache-Mojave captured in 1872 was raised by Captain James Burns and sent to Carlisle Indian School. He later wrote an invaluable autobiography (Miles, 1896).

A Cavalry patrol in Copper Canyon near the Mammoth mining camp (*Outing*, 1887).

An infantryman mounted on a mule. Contrary to popular belief, many troops in the Apache wars were infantry and were transported by any means, preferably mules (*Outing,* 1887).

General George Crook (*Outing,* 1887).

As GENERAL CROOK prepared his campaign, a special commissioner for Indian affairs, Vincent Colyer, arrived to select reservation sites. Although this delayed the campaign's start, the reservations set aside by Executive Order were far better than Stoneman's "feeding stations." Since the government could not at once furnish civilian agents to manage the Indians, Crook was allowed to install his officers and to institute wise policies for keeping the peaceful Indians content. Colyer was followed by General Oliver Otis Howard, who represented President Grant. And

again Crook's work was delayed, for Howard had authority to negotiate the return of Aravaipa Indian children—who had been sold into slavery—to relatives surviving the infamous Camp Grant Massacre in 1871. Howard also persuaded Cochise to accept a reservation, something Colyer had failed to do, and he hired Cochise's friend Tom Jeffords as agent.

Meanwhile Crook had organized three flying columns to operate against hostile Apache north and south of Camp Verde. The Chiricahua were protected from him, though they were still raiding in Mexico. In September 1872, Crook's campaign began. From then until the next April several small independent commands scoured central Arizona and fought twenty-two battles.

Major General Oliver Otis Howard, the "Christian Soldier" and hero of Gettysburg, was appointed as special Indian commissioner in 1872. He persuaded Cochise to live in peace on a huge reservation, but after Cochise's death in 1874 the reservation was reduced (Kelsey, 1901).

The reality and the myth: above is Remington's sketch of a cavalry officer in campaign dress, done from life with sombrero and gunbelt. (*Century*, 1892) . At right is the popular conception of an officer in the Indian wars, drawn by the artist R. F. Zogbaum. It is correct in all regulation details for the 1880s, including the useless saber (*Harper's Monthly*, 1890) .

Ki-at-ti-na (left) and Chi-hua-hua (*Century*, 1887).

Left and opposite page: *Ki-at-ti-na* (Looking Glass) led dissident Chiricahua in 1883 but later was a peace advocate. *Chi-hua-hua* was a leader in the 1882 outbreak from San Carlos. He later accompanied Geronimo but in 1886 he was induced to surrender by Ki-at-ti-na. *Mangas*, son of Mangas Colorado, was the last hostile leader to surrender, in 1886. *Bonito* raided with Chi-hua-hua in 1882-83. His party killed the McComas family in New Mexico.

In March 1873 the beaten tribesmen began to come into the reservations. In April the last band surrendered. Crook's policy was plain: Indians on reservations would be subsisted until self-sufficient. But off the reservation any male Indian was given one chance to surrender, then hunted down and killed. The policy worked.

General Crook, dressed in a white canvas suit and carrying a shotgun, on his mule "Apache" (*Century*, 1891).

A civilian mule packer, one of many hired by the Quartermaster Department (*Century*, 1889).

Mangas (left) and Bonito (*Century*, 1887).

A typical cavalry sergeant. The single-shot Springfield carbine attached to a snap-hook on a shoulder belt; cartridges were carried in a canvas Mills belt (*Century*, 1891).

A civilian guide sketched by Remington. The famed Al Sieber was such a scout (*Century,* 1891).

Indian scouts report to an officer wearing a pith helmet (*Outing,* 1886).

Camp San Carlos was a sub-post of Fort Apache on the reservation where scouts were recruited in the 1880s (Miles, 1896).

An Apache scout and a black trooper could get along in sign language (*Century,* 1889).

BY THE TIME the grass was up in 1874, Arizona was enjoying its first real peace in the memory of most inhabitants. In June, Cochise died. Crook had been promoted to the regular grade of brigadier general, and the following March he was called to the Northern Plains to fight the Sioux. Yet even before his departure the Indian Bureau was taking over administration of reservations; and civilian agents, such as young John P. Clum at San Carlos, were thwarting the efforts of Crook's officers. The government was bent on a policy called "concentration"; by the autumn of 1876 most bands were confined to the San Carlos reserve. Unscrupulous agents, indifferent control, dissident tribal groups, and broken promises were building a head of steam that erupted into a second war.

Hostiles observing troops with field glasses (Miles, 1896).

Apache scout, an enlisted soldier of the U.S. Army (*Century*, 1889).

Two notable scouts: Chato (inset, *Century*, 1887) helped pursue Geronimo. "Dutchy" (below, Kelsey, 1901) went with Captain Crawford into Mexico.

Officer and Apache scout reconnoitering (*Century*, 1891).

MOST OF THE SOUTHERN BAND of Chiricahua, never having known a reservation, still roamed Mexico, and in the spring of 1878 they were joined by some renegades from San Carlos. That fall about 160 of the Warm Springs band were brought from New Mexico to San Carlos. The rest of the Mimbreño in New Mexico were led by Victorio, the greatest chief since Cochise. He and his people left their reservation, cut a swathe of destruction across the territory into Arizona, and went into Sonora in 1879. In the autumn Victorio renewed his war along the border until October 1880, when he was killed in Chihuahua by Mexican soldiers. Meantime many of the renegades from San Carlos had been persuaded to return. Among them was a southern Chiricahua called Geronimo whose influence as a war leader had grown large among all the Apache. Among the Western Apache living near Fort Apache was a medicine man who inspired a ghost dance cult. In August 1881 Colonel Eugene A. Carr took a force of his 6th Cavalry and Indian scouts from the fort to Cibicue Creek to arrest the medicine man. Carr was attacked, some scouts deserted, and the troops retired to the fort.

Crook's successors: August V. Kautz (left) and Orlando B. Willcox. Kautz tried to continue his old friend's policies but ran afoul of the Indian Ring. He was replaced by Willcox in 1878; Willcox seemed oblivious to unrest and panicked in 1882 (*Appleton's*, 1889).

Colonel E. A. Carr was subordinate to Willcox. He got the blame for Cibicue; later he served under Crook with distinction (*Battles & Leaders*, 1888).

A cavalry troop pausing to drink at a desert pool (*Century*, 1889).

Crook's force that went into Mexico in 1883, drawn from a photo taken at the new town of Willcox (*Frank Leslie's Illustrated News*, 1883).

THE DEPARTMENT COMMANDER, General Orlando B. Willcox, panicked. He put all troops in the field and called for reinforcements. The excitement scared a few Indians back to the mountains; then in April 1882 the restless ones at San Carlos took advantage of the confusion to make a general exodus to Mexico led by Geronimo.

Captain Emmet Crawford, 3rd Cavalry, killed in Mexico by Mexican militia in 1886 (Kelsey, 1901).

Typical mountain terrain in Sonora (Dunn, 1886).

10th Cavalry Types

Colored troopers take their ease at evening. The sketch by Remington is marked "Sierra Bonitos—'88," which suggests a camp near Fort Grant (*Century,* 1889).

THE COMMANDING GENERAL of the army, William T. Sherman, sent Crook back to the Southwest in 1882 and gave him full authority. "The Gray Wolf," as the Indians called Crook, restored honesty to the agencies and reorganized the troops. In 1883 he pursued 400 bronco Apache south into Mexico and convinced Chato, Geronimo, and other head men that they should give up. By December, 1883, all were again domiciled at San Carlos.

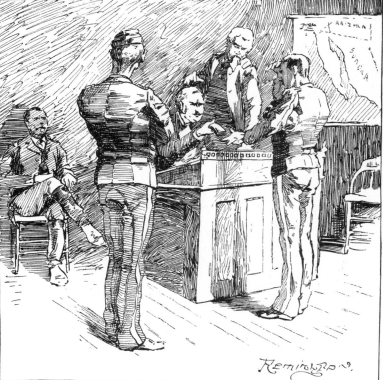

Pay day at an Arizona post. Scrubbed, shaved, and immaculate in their blue uniforms, the men report individually to the pay officer while the "old man" looks on approvingly (*Outing,* 1887).

Soldiers sketched at roll call by Remington. White troops on the frontier often included Irish and German immigrants after the Civil War (*Outing*, 1887).

GERONIMO BROKE OUT AGAIN in 1885 and was pursued into Sonora. In March, 1886 the renegades surrendered, but after a whiskey trader gave them firewater Geronimo and twenty men bolted again.

Artist Zogbaum usually painted soldiers in correct uniform. This scene might have occurred any day at guard mount at posts such as Grant and Whipple. Soldiers at remote stations regularly wore such elaborate uniforms (*Harper's Monthly*, 1890).

Cover of a dime novel by Prentiss Ingraham, published by Beadle's in 1887, portraying a black soldier. It told the adventures of a fictional "Captain Joe Bruce."

A trooper of the 10th Cavalry by Remington (*Outing*, 1887).

MORE THAN A THOUSAND Negro soldiers served in Arizona during the Indian wars, mainly in the 10th Cavalry, the Buffalo Soldiers, whose permanent home was Fort Huachuca. Other blacks were teamsters and cowboys, and at least one dime novel (above) was inspired by their presence.

GENERAL NELSON A. MILES was sent to Arizona in April 1886 to relieve Crook. He was ordered to spare no resource and make no concession in capturing Geronimo. Miles organized a hand-picked expedition led by Captain Henry Ware Lawton that doggedly pursued the hostiles. In the end, it was a handful of scouts and Lieutenant Charles B. Gatewood who caught up with them and talked Geronimo into surrendering. The Apache wars were virtually ended in September of 1886.

General Nelson A. Miles (*Century*, 1891).

Captain M. P. Maus won the Medal of Honor in the Geronimo campaign and later became a general (Miles, 1896).

Geronimo, whose Indian name was Goyathlay, was a minor figure in the 1870s but became the most feared of all Indians in the 1880s. He surrendered in 1886 and died in Oklahoma in 1909 (*Outing*, 1886).

An infantryman in field equipment of the late 1880s. Note the full-sized Springfield, Mills belt, horseshoe blanket roll, and trowel-like entrenching tool (*Century*, 1891).

A NETWORK OF HELIOGRAPH STATIONS on mountain peaks from Tucson to Lordsburg flashed messages in Morse code over hundreds of miles to facilitate the movement and supply of troops. General Miles found this device, which had been copied from British models in India, already in use when he took over the Arizona-New Mexico department.

A black trooper brings a message to headquarters in Remington's "Arrival of a Courier." The artist may have seen such an event anywhere in the Southwest where the army pursued the hostile Apache (*Century*, 1891).

A signalling station using a heliograph (Miles, 1896).

Fort Bowie was headquarters for General Crook and later for General Miles. Numbered buildings are 1-general's headquarters (dark structure at left rear of flagpole), 2-officers' quarters, 3-adjutant's office, 4-trader's store, 5-barracks, and 6-hospital. Telegraph was available at a railroad station fourteen miles away, now the town of Bowie. A heliograph station on the nearby Chiricahua Mountains provided daylight communication. Bowie was usually a "four-company" post; today it is a National Monument (*Frank Leslie's Illustrated Weekly*, 1886).

A typical troop headquarters in the field, sketched by Captain Charles A. P. Hatfield, 4th Cavalry (*Outing*, 1887).

Chiricahua Apaches at Bowie Station on the way to Florida in 1886 (Miles, 1896).

WHEN APACHE RENEGADES were jailed near a civilian community, citizens invariably tried to bring them to trial for murder or other crimes. The federal government had Geronimo's band, as well as all other Chiricahua Apache, removed to Florida rather than risk a clash of legal authority. Even the loyal scouts were exiled.

Apache prisoners in the guard house at Fort Lowell near Tucson (Bishop, 1888).

Leonard Wood won the Medal of Honor while serving as medical officer on Captain H. W. Lawton's expedition into Mexico. He later was colonel of Roosevelt's Rough Riders (Miles, 1896).

VI. COMMERCE AND INDUSTRY

A mining camp in Arizona (Shearer, 1884).

By 1879 Arizona's name was synonymous with silver, but that status was illusory. As everyone knew that Sonora was one big silver mine, it was assumed that Arizona, lately a part of Sonora, must possess untold wealth. Silver mines were eagerly reopened after they had been abandoned, and ancient copper deposits were reworked. But hostile Indians, lack of transportation, and finally the Civil War frustrated development.

Prospectors loading mules with camp gear; the men at the rear are having trouble (Conklin, 1878).

A ton of silver cast as ingots (*Harper's Monthly*, 1878).

The rocker was a simple way of separating gold from gravel. It was a box with a perforated bottom, mounted on rockers like a baby's cradle. Water was poured in and the machine rocked vigoriously. Riffles in a trough underneath caught the grains of gold (Elliott, 1884). Above, right, "A Miner's Vicissitudes in Arizona" (Conklin, 1878).

IN 1857 DISAPPOINTED goldseekers from California began to cross the Rio Colorado, and two years later Gila City sprang up around some placers. Similar surface deposits were soon found at La Paz and Quartzsite, and all were quickly exhausted by miners using the pan and cradle or rocker.

One primitive method of winnowing gold from pay dirt was through use of a pan in a stream of water to separate gold from sand and gravel. The Mexicans originated panning (Thayer, 1888).

The primitive *arrastra* ore crusher was borrowed from Mexico. A mule dragged a crushing stone around a pivot post. Sometimes several mules and more stones were used. For details, see next page (Browne, 1869).

Pure gold found in loose gravel was mined by "placering" if water was at hand. Miners diverted a steady stream into a sluice, then shoveled in the pay dirt. Riffles in the bottom caught large metallic pieces, and a blanket at the end caught the finest particles of gold (*Century*, 1882).

IN 1862 A PARTY of prospectors from New Mexico discovered gold on the headwaters of the Hassayampa River. A rush started to Lynx Creek, to Granite Creek, and into the Bradshaw Mountains, bringing with it the new territorial government. The Weaver, Oatman, and Castle Dome districts were also opened.

Arizona miners often went to extremes to secure water. In the late 1880s Alexander O. Brodie built a large dam on the Hassayampa River. Shown here are two 25-inch delivery pipes for hydraulic mining. When nearly completed in 1890, the dam burst with tragic loss of life (*Scribner's*, 1890).

Closeup of the primitive Mexican arrastra, showing stone slab walls, paving, and method of attaching stones. Water was added to the ore (De Quille, 1877).

The Toltec mining camp in Pima County was near the venerable Salero Mine. It flourished about two years (Hinton, 1878).

The town and mine called Silver King was located in 1875 near the present site of Superior. After a corporation was formed in 1878, the mine produced over $1,500,000 in dividends to stockholders (Hamilton, 1884).

BY THE END of the Civil War it was evident that when mining went underground there was more silver than gold to be found. In 1873 a national depression and a halt in silver coinage dashed hopes of wealth, yet in that same year Globe's silver deposits were discovered. Silver became legal tender in 1878, and simultaneously Ed Schieffelin and partners staked the Tombstone District claims. The boom began the following year, and Tombstone proved to be Arizona's only bonanza.

Crude ladders found in old Spanish mines indicate that Arizona has a longer history of mining than any other state (Hinton, 1878).

The Ingersoll rock drill ran by compressed air or steam. Advertisements claimed that "one small drill . . . will do more work . . . than nine men could do, provided so many could find room to work there at once" (Ingham, 1880).

AFTER THE WAR it was the anticipation of finding new silver lodes that attracted entrepreneurs to the territory, and along with them the merchants, freighters, and agriculturists who shortly outnumbered the miners. After Tombstone, however, about the only rich finds were of gold, the purchasing power of which increased sharply in the '80s. Even

today gold is an important by-product of copper smelting, and Arizona ranks fourth in gold production. The amount of copper had always been suspect. No one knew how long it had been mined at Ajo, and in 1864 Henry Clifton discovered native outcrops on the San Francisco River. Many veins of gold and silver were accompanied by copper. As Apache trouble subsided, some high grade ore could be mined. In the 1880s railroads and new extraction processes permitted miners to develop the first of Arizona's "three C's": Copper, Cattle, and Cotton.

Gila City as seen by J. Ross Browne in 1864 had "three chimneys and a coyote." The town sprang up after discovery of placer gold in 1858, about 24 miles from Yuma. Over 1,000 people arrived inside three months, but the town was abandoned when the "color" played out (Browne, 1869).

Schematic view of a "leaching and amalgamating works" for reducing silver and copper ores. Copper was leached by steeping ore in weak sulphuric acid, producing copper sulphate which reacted with scrap iron to produce copper (Hinton, 1878).

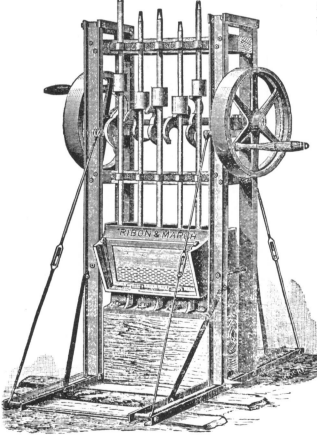

A gravity stamp mill advertised as portable yet "capable of crushing ordinary hard quartz rock on sixty 6-inch drops per minute." Cams dropped the stamps in succession; the pulverized ore fell through a screen. The mill weighed a ton but could be dismantled into mule loads (*Engineering and Mining Journal,* 1881).

Cutaway of an amalgamating pan. Stamp mills were also sometimes used for amalgamating (*Harper's Monthly,* 1878).

ALTHOUGH ALL hard-rock mining was difficult. the techniques for extracting high-grade copper were not much different than for gold and silver. The smelting and refining of copper ores, however, required enormous capital and transportation facilities. In 1880 Dr. James Douglas was engaged by the New York firm of Phelps, Dodge and Company to see if an investment in the Clifton mines was wise. Douglas, who had extensive scientific training, studied the Arizona picture and advised investment, not only at Clifton but also in the Copper Queen at Bisbee. Thus Phelps,

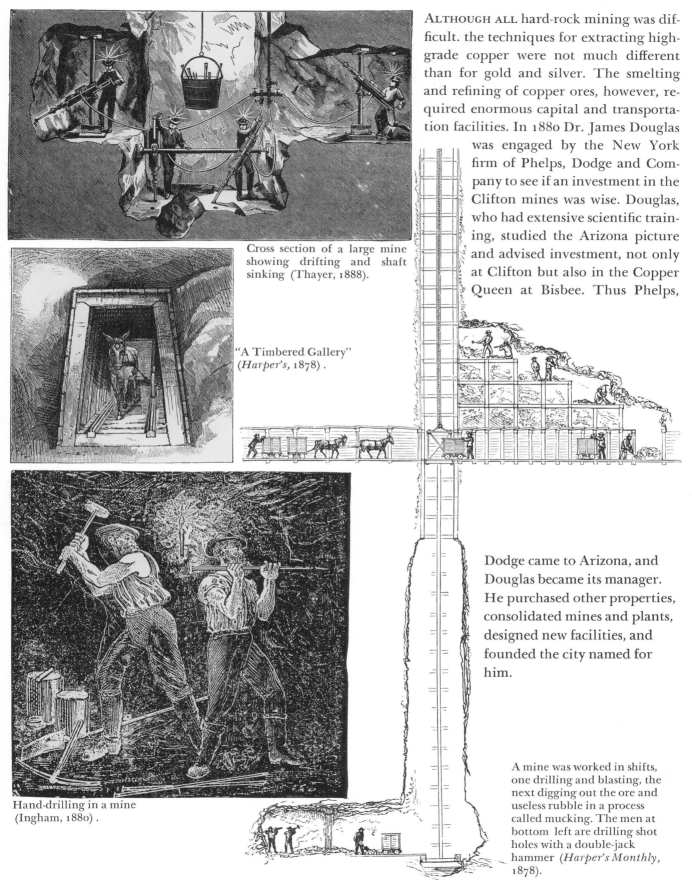

Cross section of a large mine showing drifting and shaft sinking (Thayer, 1888).

"A Timbered Gallery" (*Harper's*, 1878) .

Dodge came to Arizona, and Douglas became its manager. He purchased other properties, consolidated mines and plants, designed new facilities, and founded the city named for him.

Hand-drilling in a mine (Ingham, 1880) .

A mine was worked in shifts, one drilling and blasting, the next digging out the ore and useless rubble in a process called mucking. The men at bottom left are drilling shot holes with a double-jack hammer (*Harper's Monthly*, 1878).

A rock-boring machine powered by steam or air (Thayer, 1888).

The richest copper mine in territorial days was the United Verde, though it is now closed and the town of Jerome is a ghost (opposite page, Elliott, 1884). The ore body was discovered in 1876, but it was six years before a company was organized by Eugene M. Jerome. It produced $800,000 worth of copper in one year. In 1888 the property was leased by William Andrews Clark, the Montana copper king, who purchased it the next year, built a larger smelter, and laid his own railway to connect with the Santa Fe. Phelps Dodge later acquired the United Verde, after Clark had amassed

Mouth of a mine tunneled into solid rock, requiring little shoring and with easy access for rail cars (Ingham, 1880).

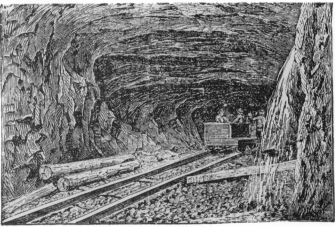

a fortune. When the operation ended in 1953, it was estimated to have produced copper and metals valued at half a billion dollars.

Extraction of copper from porphyry ores was a puzzle until 1899 when experiments in Utah promised a practical solution. Promptly old and new companies began their own experiments; the Calumet and Arizona Company's experiments were especially notable and they purchased some old mines at Ajo in 1902. The high grade copper had long since been carted away, but under a former Rough Rider, Colonel John C. Greenway, the New Cornelia Mine became a paying producer. By the time the Ajo interests merged in 1930, the plant had produced 345 million pounds.

Mines usually were drifted and stoped into ground that alternated loose earth with rock. They required expensive timbers and hoisting apparatus (Thayer, 1888).

United Verde Copper Company's works at Jerome. At lower right is the opening of the Eureka Mine; at upper left are openings to the tunnels of the Chrome Mine (Elliott, 1884).

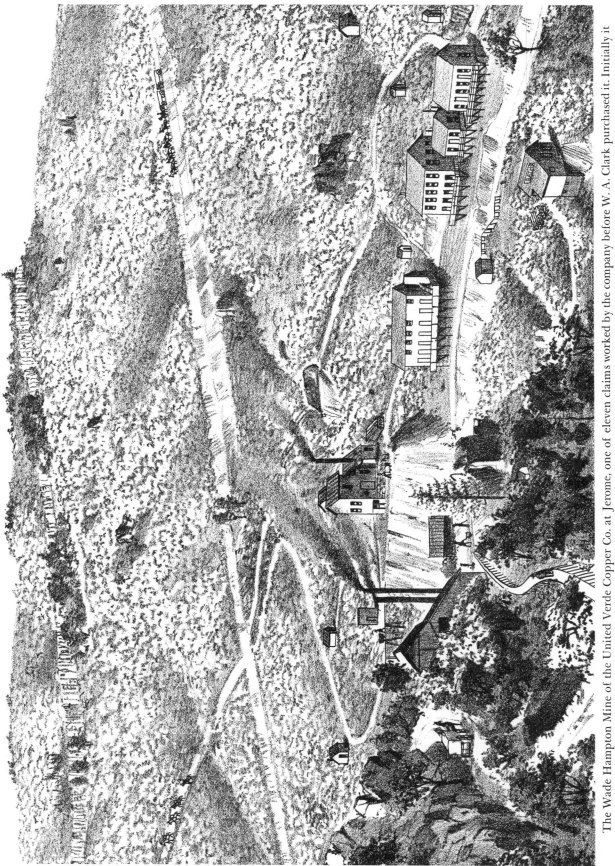

The Wade Hampton Mine of the United Verde Copper Co. at Jerome, one of eleven claims worked by the company before W. A. Clark purchased it. Initially it tapped the same vein as the nearby Eureka Mine, but later the Hampton had to sink a shaft and put in the hoisting works seen here (Elliott, 1884).

A silver mill using the wet process—the major type in Arizona. The process involved wet crushing, followed by amalgamation with mercury in pans and separators (*Harper's* 1878).

A silver mill using the dry process, by which silver ore containing other metals such as copper was crushed while dry, roasted, and passed on to the amalgamator (*Harper's* 1878).

The mills of two mines in the Turkey Creek District near Prescott: the Hidden Treasure and the Wonder, treating both gold and silver ores (Hamilton. 1884).

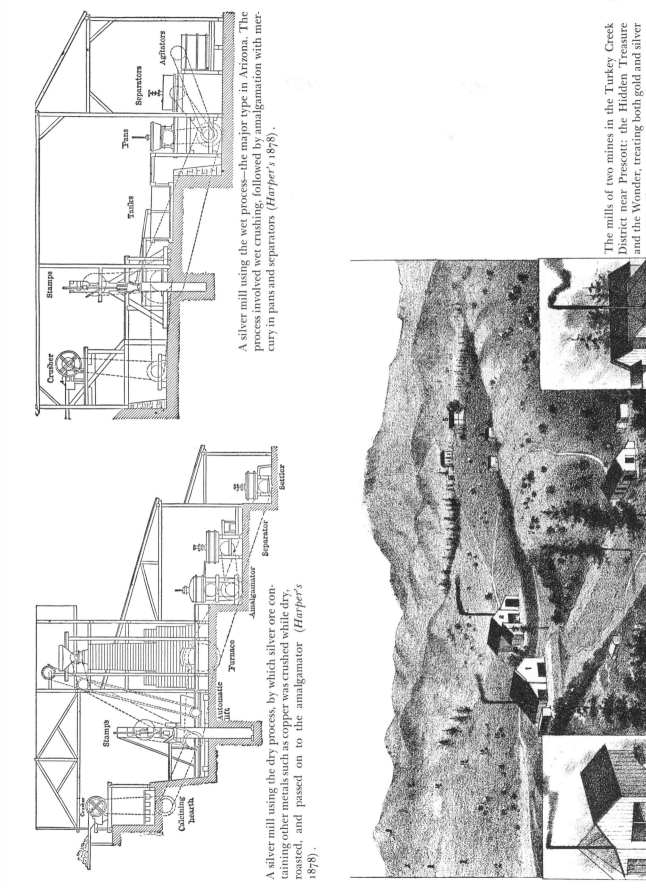

Prospector discovering gold accidentally while deer hunting. At least one Arizona mine, the Cazador, was named this way (Thayer, 1888).

Ed Schieffelin discovered silver instead of his tombstone near the Dragoon Mountains (Bishop, 1888).

THE RISE OF THE OPEN RANGE cattle industry paralleled the development of mining in Arizona, and this was no coincidence. Miners had to eat, and beef was the chief bill-of-fare. Prior to the Civil War, ranching had been only a continuance of the Mexican style of ranching with small herds of native cattle and some few Texas herds that were diverted from the drives to California. After the war attempts were made to stock the ranges of southern Arizona with Texas longhorns, but Indian depredations discouraged ranchers until Crook brought peace in 1873. Following 1873 any halfway skillful cowman could turn a good profit selling beef cattle to the army posts and Indian agencies, as well as to the mines.

Charles McMillen and Josiah Flournoy, two well-known Arizona miners. McMillen found the rich Stonewall Jackson silver mine in 1874, sold it for $120,000 within months, and then tapped the same ledge with other mines. His partner was Flournoy (Conklin, 1878).

William F. "Buffalo Bill" Cody invested heavily in the Campo Bonito mine near Tucson and often visited his property (Kelsey, 1901).

Remington's picture, "Stockmen Looking over a New Range," could be anywhere in the West of the 1880s. Arizona attracted cowmen from other states, such as John H. Slaughter and Jesse W. Ellison from Texas, William Wingfield from Oregon, George T. Peter of Colorado, and Eastern and foreign men (*Century*, 1888).

A *vaquero* of the Borderlands, such as Remington saw in Chihuahua and Arizona (*Century*, 1888).

Trailing cattle in new herds to Arizona before railroads. First came the longhorns; later cattlemen imported blooded stock such as Herefords (*Century*, 1888).

WILLIAM S. OURY, whose ranch was south of Tucson, brought the first pureblood cattle in 1868. Four years later, Henry Clay Hooker founded the Sierra Bonita Ranch in the Sulphur Springs Valley and he introduced purebred horses. When the railroads came in the 1880s, new cattle kingdoms arose along the routes. Small ranchers in the country between the railroads suffered through the last Apache wars.

Branding a horse
(*Century*, 1888).

The "remuda" or horse herd of a cow outfit, held in a rope corral ready to be saddled for the day's work (*Century*, 1888).

Roping in a horse corral
(*Century*, 1888).

Saddling fresh horses. The Arizona open-range cattle industry boomed as silver mining declined. Railroads offered a way to market and the army bought beef for troops and for several thousand newly corraled Indians (*Century*, 1888).

Cutting a steer out of the herd. Arizona was advertised as a new El Dorado where "grass was free and law was lax." By 1891 Arizona was home for over 720,000 cattle (*Century*, 1888).

Branding calves in a corral (Thayer, 1888).

A large old-time brand (Thayer, 1888).

THE MOST AMBITIOUS Arizona ranch was the short-lived Aztec Land & Cattle Co., using the Hashknife brand. The company shipped 38,000 head of cattle from Texas to graze along 1,700 square miles of a railroad land grant. Overgrazing, drought, theft, and other troubles made the ranch unprofitable; it lasted seven years.

Remington's sketch of "A Hard Trail" (*Century*, 1888).

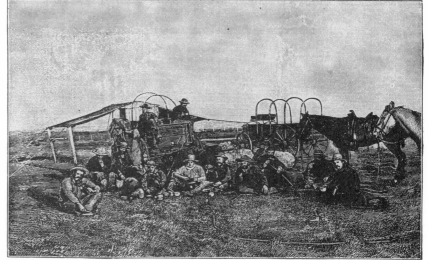

The chuck wagon was a rolling commissary that accompanied drives and roundups (Thayer, 1888).

An Arizona cowboy
(*Century*, 1888).

Pulling down a steer. The puncher is taking a "dally" with his lariat around the saddle horn before dismounting (*Century* 1888).

A dispute over a brand
(*Century*, 1888).

Part of a front page of a weekly newspaper published in Tucson by Colin and Brewster Cameron, themselves proprietors of the San Rafael Ranch. Ranchers publicized their brands, as legal notices and to recover stray stock (Elliott, 1884).

By the early 1890s, overgrazing, erosion, and droughts drastically reduced range herds. Ranches folded; many could survive only if they fenced, planted, and pumped. Purebred steers were raised instead of longhorns; large companies ranched more efficiently; only a few old territorial ranchers survived.

A sulky plow (Thayer, 1888).

Irrigating alfalfa by flooding in the Salt River Valley (*Scribner's*, 1890).

Farm scene in Kirkland Valley southwest of Prescott (Elliott, 1884).

A camp of sheepmen en route to their winter range (Bureau of Animal Husbandry, 1892).

Sheep shearing (Thayer, 1888).

SHEEP WERE NOT NEGLECTED in Arizona, as Merinos and other purebreds were imported to northern ranges. At least one cattle company, the Babbitt brothers of Flagstaff, ran both sheep and cattle successfully. Sheep sometimes created problems for small ranchers, and disputes over range and water rights led to bloody clashes. In the 1880s a deadly range war in the Pleasant Valley took ninety lives. Claims to public domain by homesteaders, not all of them sheepmen, also broke up the open range.

Two splendid homes in the farming settlement of Mesa: that of John Pomeroy (far left), a member of the legislature, and that of Daniel Bagley. By the time Mesa was incorporated in 1883 is was the richest agricultural region in the territory (Elliott, 1884).

Saddling an ornery cow pony in an Arizona corral. Note the double-rig, Texas-style stock saddle, and the stirrups with hoods or *tapaderos*. This familiar picture is usually assumed to represent a Texas or Montana scene, yet Remington placed some saguaro cactus on the hills (*Century*, 1888).

A stagecoach on Colonel Chidester's line about to leave Fort Worth for Fort Concho, Texas, 1879. At Fort Concho it connected with the San Antonio and El Paso mail line, successor to the old Butterfield line, en route to Yuma over the former Overland Mail road (*Harper's Monthly,* 1879).

AFTER THE MEXICAN WAR, visionaries dreamed of a railroad to the Pacific. Instead, Arizona got the Great Overland Mail Road and stagecoaches. In 1857 the Post Office awarded the overland mail contract to John Butterfield of New York. At a cost of one million dollars he strung a line of nearly 200 stations from Tipton, Missouri, to San Francisco via Yuma with almost 2,000 men, 500 coaches and 1,500 head of horses and mules, and in September, 1858 began to run stages.

John Butterfield, organizer of the Overland Mail Company (University of California).

A celerity wagon, often used between El Paso and Fort Yuma (James, 1906).

ARIZONA MAIL & STAGE CO

CARRIES U. S. MAIL AND WELLS, FARGO & CO'S EXPRESS

Fare to or from Fairbank, $1.50.

Leaves Tombstone at 7:15 a. m. to connect with Trains for Nogales, Bisbee and all points South   Arrives in Tombstone 11:00 A. M.

Leaves Tombstone at 1:45 p. m. for Fairbank to connect with trains at Benson for all points East and West

BAGGAGE of Passengers delivered to and from Stage office in the city Free of Charge

Advertisement in the Tombstone Epitaph, 1886. The inaccurate picture is a stock cut used all over the West. Wells, Fargo & Co. never operated its own coaches in Arizona but used other lines.

Below, a typical light coach generally used throughout Arizona (James, 1906).

Stagecoach robbery in Arizona, an all too common event where coaches carried bullion from the mines (Conklin, 1878).

An Arizona stage station (Gleed, 1882).

A coach passing Lone Peaks (somewhat exaggerated) on the road between Ehrenberg and Wickenburg (Shearer, 1884).

The coach of the Arizona Mail & Stage Co. before the Occidental Hotel in Tombstone. Numerous travelers with money inspired good lines between Tombstone, Benson, and Tucson. Elsewhere travel was primitive (Elliott, 1884).

IN APRIL 1861, the Overland Mail was shifted to the Central Route and Arizona was without scheduled service until regular connections with California resumed in 1867. After 1869, when the Union Pacific transcontinental railroad was completed, Arizonans watched the rail lines compete for control of the Southwest.

A six-mule team and freight wagon. The three views on this page (all from *Outing*, 1887) show how to get there by mule. Stagecoaches were usually mule-powered as well.

The army often used light wagons with a four-mule team.

A packer tightening a cinch on a government mule. One mule could carry 400 pounds all day.

UNTIL THE RAILROADS CAME, Arizonans rode stagecoaches and financed mulepowered freight lines. Huge, high-sided wagons drawn by a dozen or more mules hauled ore, hides and wool, food-stuffs and whiskey, grand pianos and clothing.

"The Red Man's Parcel Post," by Frederic Remington (*Harper's Monthly*, 1895).

FIVE RAIL COMPANIES vied for rights to build across Arizona, but in the spring of 1877 the Southern Pacific of California was closest as it reached Fort Yuma. The Southern Pacific obtained a right-of-way from a grateful territorial legislature and by 1880 had laid its tracks over the Gila Trail to Tucson. Deming, New Mexico was connected a year later. Meanwhile the Atlantic and Pacific Company had entered Arizona from Albuquerque along Beale's camel road. The Atlantic and Pacific reached Flagstaff in 1882, and late the next summer was stopped at the Colorado River; the Southern Pacific held the right-of-way on the opposite shore. The Atchison, Topeka and Santa Fe Railroad later absorbed the Atlantic and Pacific and penetrated California. It was 1895 before one could ride through from Ashfork on the Santa Fe in the north to Nogales on the Mexican border. For many years after the Southern Pacific reached Yuma and bought out the steam navigation company, steamboats continued to carry goods upriver for Prescott and the northern mines and ranches. By and large, freighting firms hauled the goods of commerce and industry. Arizona still relied greatly on animal-drawn transportation as the twentieth century dawned.

A light stage abandoned on the desert (James, 1906).

THE TELEGRAPH REACHED Arizona from California in 1873 as a military project, although it was always available to civilian use at cost. Not for almost ten more years could Arizonans send telegrams directly east. In northern Arizona the telegraph came with the railroad in 1882. The coming of the railroad also opened valuable timber lands as a new industry, and Edward E. Ayer, Minnesota lumber king who had been a soldier in Arizona during the Civil War, built a mill at Flagstaff in 1881 ahead of the railroad. It later supplied ties for construction in Mexico.

General Nelson Miles writing a message in the telegraph office at Bowie Station (Miles, 1896).

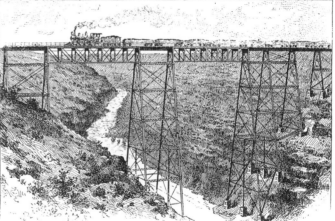

The yard of the Arizona Lumber and Timber Co., about 1890 (Ayer Collection).

The Atlantic & Pacific (later Santa Fe) railroad bridge across Canyon Diablo, 35 miles east of Flagstaff. Built in 1882, it is one of the most spectacular bridges in the West (Higgins, 1895).

An early wood-burning locomotive of the type used on early Arizona lines (Adv., 1880).

Red Rock Pass above Yuma, with Chimney Peak in the distance. Before dams were built, there were several landings where goods were transferred (Conklin, 1878).

Norton's Landing on the Colorado, 52 miles upriver from Yuma (Bishop, 1888).

Carl Schuchard's lithograph of Fort Yuma shows the steamer *General Jesup* in 1854. The vessel supplied the fort, was 108 feet long and drew only 30 inches of water. The only other sidewheeler ever used was the *Uncle Sam*, a 65-foot boat that sank in 1853 (Gray, 1856).

Robinson's Landing at the mouth of the Colorado. Although Mexican territory, this site and the nearby Port Isabel were thriving entrepots for American goods that came by sea up the Gulf of California. Ocean steamships unloaded cargoes onto lighters, which in turn took passengers and freight to waiting steamboats. Here also Lieutenant Ives assembled his *Explorer* in 1857 (Ives, 1861).

Ives' "Railroad Pass." This gateway between the Cerbat Mountains on the north and the Hualpai Mountains to the south was first used by Father Garces in 1776. Lieutenant Ives crossed in 1858 and recommended it for railroad use. In 1883 the Atlantic & Pacific laid their tracks through it to the Colorado (Ives, 1861).

The railway bridge at Needles on the Colorado (Higgins, 1911).

The village of Flagstaff was first an emigrant camp on the Beale Road, then a supply point for railroad construction. When E. E. Ayer established a lumber mill in 1881, the town prospered (Hamilton, 1884).

VII. TOWNS

Tucson in the 1880s, viewed from the west. In the foreground are adobe ruins of the mission school abandoned in the 1820s (Hamilton, 1884).

Burros loaded with mesquite fire-wood (Sweetser, 1892).

Pima County courthouse, built in 1893 (Dawn collection).

Tucson, a Piman name for a place at the foot of a dark hill, was an Indian village on the west side of the Rio Santa Cruz near Sentinel Peak. In August of 1775 Don Hugo O'Conor of the King's army chose a site on a low mesa just east of the river for a new presidio whence the Tubac garrison was transferred the next year. Franciscan priests from San Xavier began a mission school around the turn of the century. Until 1856 San Agustín del Tucson was a walled fort with a few soldiers' families, friendly Indians, and merchants. In 1867 the territorial government was moved to Tucson where the Capital remained for ten years. In 1871 the townsite was incorporated and nine years later the population was 7,000.

Tucson in 1864. The large flag in the plaza indicates occupation by California troops. A year later the camp was moved to the east edge of town and in 1866 was named for Brigadier General Charles R. Lowell (Browne, 1869).

The Carleton Meteorite discovered about 1853 by a Tucson blacksmith, Ramon Pacheco, who used the 632-pound object as an anvil (Bartlett, 1854).

A Tucson street scene in the 1880s (Bishop. 1888).

TUCSON REMAINED until 1880 mainly a stopping place on the crossroads to California and Sonora, with nearby Fort Lowell to support Indian campaigns. The transformation to a modern city began with establishment of a landgrant college in 1894, and copper mines and cotton farms brought wealth. By 1910 Tucson had 13,000 people.

Among the giant cacti in what is now the Saguaro National Monument (Lummis, 1892).

Residence of Thomas Fitch in Tucson, 1881. He is said to have paid $20,000 for this house, which had hollow walls to circulate cool air, a 4,000-gallon cistern, and leathered wallpaper (Elliott, 1884).

Tom Fitch, "the silver-tongued orator," was a former Nevada congressman who moved to Prescott in 1878 and later to Tucson. He urged a lottery to raise school funds (Elliott, 1884).

The Santa Rita Hotel in Tucson, as it looked in 1912. It is still in business, favored by stockmen (Dawn Collection).

J. Knox Corbett Lumber Company, about 1900 (Dawn Collection).

Tucson in the 1890s (Sweetser, 1892).

The store of Louis Zeckendorf at Main and Pennington in Tucson. The Zeck-endorfs had valuable mercantile and mining interests in New Mexico as well. A relative, Albert Steinfeld, later founded a leading Tucson store (Elliott, 1884).

F. Ronstadt Company's farm machinery store and wagon shop sold everything from buggies to plows and also did blacksmithing (courtesy W. A. Duffen).

The M. G. Roca store on Main Street was begun by a native of Chile in 1860 (Gleed, 1882).

Prescott, then capital of Arizona. Fort Whipple, just outside town, was headquarters for an area as far as San Diego (Hinton, 1878).

One printer used a stock cut showing false fronts and labeled it Prescott (Gleed, 1882).

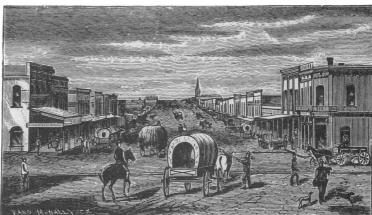

The Prescott public school, built in 1876 for 300 scholars (Gleed, 1885).

PRESCOTT, named for the historian William Hickling Prescott, was founded by the territorial government in April, 1864. Governor Goodwin thereby acknowledged that most of the white population north of the Gila was in that vicinity. The capital was returned from Tucson in 1877 to remain for a dozen more years. The town had no railroad connection until 1887. Since 1890, it has been a mining and ranching center. In 1900 the wooden stores were nearly wiped out by fire; by 1910 Prescott had 5,000 people.

Samuel Carson Miller, wagon freighter, rancher, and Indian fighter (Elliott, 1884).

The Bank of Arizona at the corner of Gurley and Cortez streets in Prescott (Hinton, 1878).

Home of S. C. Miller, on Miller Creek just north of Prescott. Originally from Illinois, Miller came to Arizona with the Walker prospecting expedition in 1862 (Elliott, 1884).

Yavapai County courthouse. Built of brick and stone, it was said to be the finest in the territory in the 1880s. It stood until 1924 (Hamilton, 1884).

Residence of Charles B. Rush in Prescott. He came from Missouri via California as a stockraiser in 1877 and was later a district attorney (Elliott, 1884).

View of Prescott from the northeast in the early 1880s (Hamilton, 1884).

PHOENIX BEGAN IN 1867 when Jack Swilling formed an irrigation company. The town was named Phoenix in 1869 and soon absorbed another community around Helling's flour mill to the east. In 1889 it became the territory's capital. When Arizona became a state in 1912 the metropolitan area had 20,000 people, including adjoining Mesa and Tempe.

Early street scene in Phoenix (Hinton, 1878).

National Bank of Arizona in the 1890s (Dawn Collection).

Adams Hotel in the 1890s (Dawn Collection).

Old city hall on Washington and First streets, used as a capitol in 1889 (Sweetser, 1892).

The Irvine Building on Washington and Montezuma streets (Elliott, 1884).

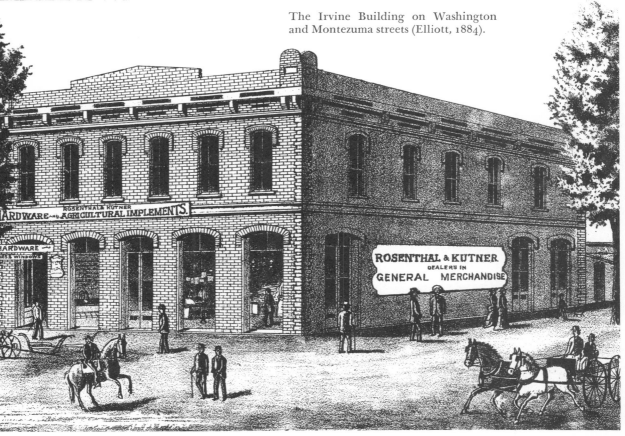

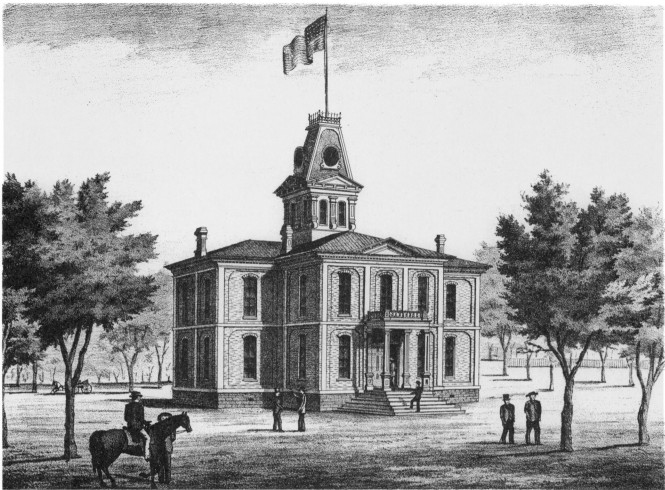

The Maricopa County courthouse. The county was created from Yavapai in 1871 and enlarged at the expense of Pima County two years later. The courthouse was built in 1884 (Elliott, 1884).

Architect's drawing of the Arizona Capitol, begun in 1899 and occupied the following year. The dome is, of course, of copper. It was designed by a San Antonio architect (courtesy Arizona State Library).

The Phoenix public school, a two-story brick building (Hamilton, 1884).

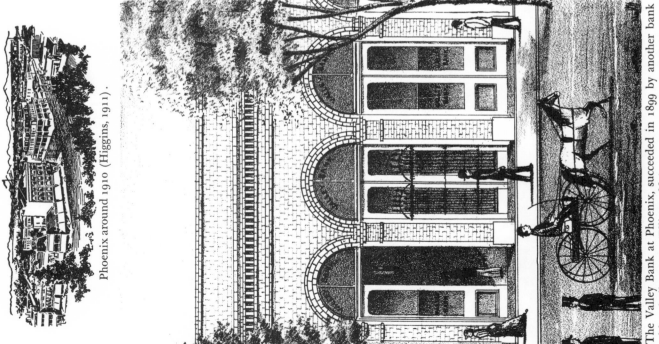

Phoenix around 1910 (Higgins, 1911).

The Valley Bank at Phoenix, succeeded in 1899 by another bank with a similar name (Elliott, 1884).

Churches and other views in Phoenix (Elliott, 1884).

The jail at St. Johns, Apache County seat. This stockraising center began with a bridge across the Little Colorado in 1872; Mormon colonists began the actual settlement around 1880. Except for the jail, nearly all buildings were of adobe (Hamilton, 1884).

View down the canyon of the San Francisco River where the town of Clifton was settled around 1873. Patrick Hamilton called it "the typical Arizona mining camp." It may have been named for Henry Clifton, who found copper here, or for the cliffs above the town (Hamilton, 1884).

FLORENCE WAS ONE OF THE FIRST settlements in Pinal County, a mercantile center for an extensive ranching and mining region begun in 1866. It is said to have been named for a sister of Governor A. P. K. Safford. In the 1880s it rivaled Tucson and the census of 1890 showed 1,500 residents. Today it remains the county seat with many interesting old buildings.

A Florence street lined with cottonwoods, irrigated by ditches (Hinton, 1878).

Store of José M. Ochoa, native of Sonora. A majority of Florence citizens were Spanish-speaking (Elliott, 1884).

Pinal County courthouse, which provided offices and courtroom and housed prisoners as well. Today it is occupied by the Pinal County Historical Society (Elliott, 1884).

Feed yard and saloon in Florence owned by J. V. Wilson. Upstairs hall was home of the Ancient Order of United Workmen (Elliott, 1884).

Peter Will's brewery in Florence. Every important town had at least one brewery which supplied homemade "lager" and served as a social hall (Elliott, 1884).

ABOUT 1858 TWO TOWNS began on the Arizona side of the Colorado across from Fort Yuma. One was L. J. F. Iaeger's ferry terminus called Colorado City, the home of mescal peddlers, shady ladies, and a few merchants. Nearby upstream was Arizona City, which gained the post office in 1864. By 1870 more than 1,100 persons lived on the south side and were calling their community Yuma.

George A. Johnson's ferry landing in Arizona at Yuma Crossing. The ferry was hauled by the stationary steam engine in right foreground. Several wagon teams are seen waiting to embark while one of Johnson's steamboats unloads at the store of Hooper and Hinton. Fort Yuma is seen across the river in California (courtesy Arizona Pioneers' Historical Society).

The Colorado near Yuma during the spring flood season, often disastrous until dams upstream controlled the river (Gleed, 1885).

THE YUMA COUNTY SEAT was moved to Yuma from La Paz in 1870. The busy river port already had an army supply depot, and in 1876 the territorial prison was opened. Next year came the railroad which sharply curtailed river traffic. Mining declined in the 1880s. As the twentieth century dawned, Yuma had a population of 2,900 and was becoming an agricultural center. It is still a welcome stopping place for east-west travelers.

A street in old Yuma (James, 1906).

Yuma in the 1880s, looking across the river from the south (Gleed, 1882).

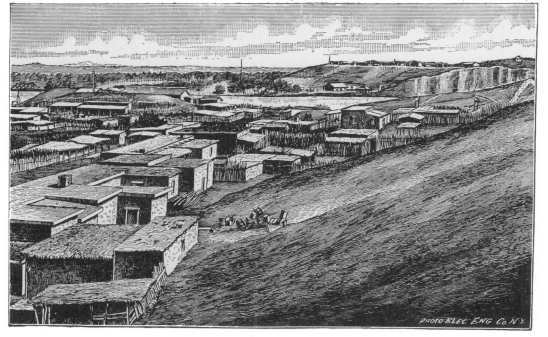

Indians playing hoop and pole game at Ehrenberg. Michael Goldwater opened a store in 1860, and the town was an important river point after the gold played out (Gleed, 1885).

Ehrenberg had only 500 people by 1871 (Gleed, 1885).

The Southern Pacific Railroad bridge at Yuma, seen from the California side. This wooden structure was built in 1877 and re-placed by a steel structure in 1915 (Hamilton, 1884).

Tombstone in its heyday, 1884. By that time it had passed through two disastrous fires (Hamilton, 1884).

ABOVE THE TUNNELS of the Toughnut and Lucky Cuss mines on the northern spurs of the Mule Mountains arose a shanty town called Tombstone. The first house went up in 1879. The indifferent miners had their camp swept twice by fires before a permanent town arose in 1882. About this time its population was over 5,000 and it was the seat of Cochise County. One mine, the Contention, produced over five million dollars. Then the silver decline reduced the camp to a mere 646 souls by 1900. It lost the county seat to Bisbee in 1931, but the old courthouse is a state monument and museum.

A distant view of Tombstone, with the Mule Mountains on the horizon (Bishop, 1888).

The Occidental Hotel in Tombstone, 1885 (Dawn Collection).

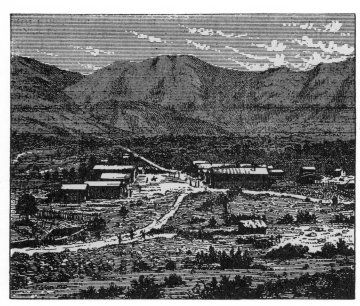

The mining camp of Mineral Park in Cerbat Basin northwest of Kingman. In 1872 silver was discovered and a town of 700 sprang up. The Keystone Mine produced $100,000 in 1884, but nearby Kingman became the county seat when the railroad went through Mohave County. Mineral Park became a ghost town (Hinton, 1878).

The Nogales public school, built in 1899. Two early citizens were Jacob Isaacson, postmaster, and Isaac N. Town, a ranch manager. The town was called variously Isaacson, Isaactown, Line City, and Nogales (*Arizona Graphic*, 1899).

The Cerbat Basin between the Black Mountains and the Cerbat Range (Ives, 1861).

Charles Banker's Brewery, Globe (Elliott, 1884). Since 1873 Globe's copper and silver mines have produced over a billion dollars.

Residence and restaurant of J. H. Pascoe, Globe City (Elliott, 1884).

View on Main Street, Globe, with J. H. Hyndman's hotel at right (Elliott, 1884). In the center is the office of the *Arizona Silver Belt*, a leading territorial newspaper. The building also housed the U.S. post office.

Lowell Observatory in Flagstaff; the first telescope was installed in 1894 (Higgins, 1911).

Flagstaff in 1910, looking north (Higgins, 1911).

"Flagstaff," said an observer in 1884, has a "half dozen stores and as many saloons." Above is the store of P. B. Brannen & Co. at the corner of Santa Fe St. and San Francisco Ave. Today the site is occupied by a saloon (Elliott, 1884).

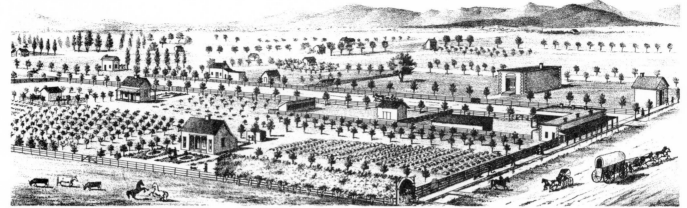

The farm of A. F. MacDonald, president of the Mormon Maricopa Stake in 1882. At right are the relief society hall, a hotel, and the Mesa City Store—start of the town of Mesa in 1878 (Elliott, 1884).

MORMON SETTLEMENT in Arizona began in the 1870s at such places as Mesa City, Snowflake, and Pipe Spring. With support from Utah, carefully selected leaders planted orderly, self-sufficient colonies along water courses for irrigation or in grasslands that could support livestock. Wheat, beef, wool, and cheese boosted Arizona's economy.

Erastus Snow, who with William J. Flake founded the stock-raising center of Snowflake in 1879 (Andrew Jenson Collection).

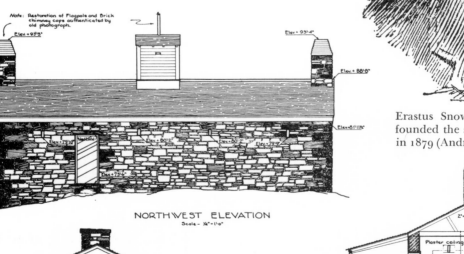

NORTHWEST ELEVATION
Scale - ¼" = 1'-0"

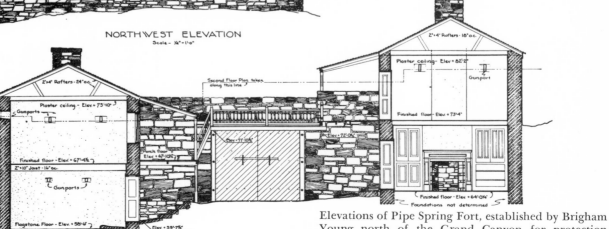

Elevations of Pipe Spring Fort, established by Brigham Young north of the Grand Canyon for protection against Navajo (National Park Service, 1941).

VIII. TERRITORIAL LIFE

The *baile* was a common
pastime of Mexican days,
accompanied by guitars and
presided over by sober *dueñas*
(*Outing*, 1886).

OUR PIONEERING PREDECESSORS were more intent on extracting mineral wealth and utilizing timber and grass than they were in permanent settlement. Arizona until the 1890s was a land of mining camps, army posts, and lonely ranches, dominated by dauntless prospectors, duelling journalists, itinerant merchants, and quick-triggered cattlemen. When silver mining declined and copper became a long term proposition for outside capitalists; and when the army departed, removing a captive market for the goods and vices of a frontier economy, Arizonans turned to intensive crop agriculture and to stabilized stockraising. Territorial life became rural and placid.

Horse racing was a favorite sport in Arizona from the earliest times (*Outing*, 1887).

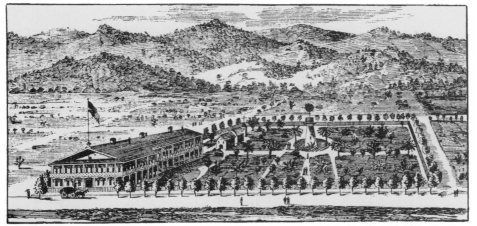

Plan of C. P. Sykes' hotel at Calabasas "as it will appear when completed" (*Daily Graphic*, 1878). Sykes hoped to sell surrounding acreage of his Mexican grant. The hotel opened in 1882.

Flamboyant promotion claimed this ear of corn grew near Calabasas in 1876 "without irrigation, 12 inches long" (*Daily Graphic*, 1878).

Colonel Charles P. Sykes, a mining promoter whose enemies said he claimed the Santa Cruz river was navigable. In 1894 his land claim was voided. (*Daily Graphic*, 1878).

George J. Roskruge of Tucson, one of the most successful Arizona mappers. Surveyors were important men in territorial days (Dawn Collection).

A triangulation station for use of a transit in mapping (Powell, 1895).

Roosevelt Dam on the Salt River under construction in 1906 (Dawn Collection).

The Walnut Grove dam built by Alexander O. Brodie on the Has-sayampa River. It was 110 feet high and 410 feet wide and had impounded a lake a half mile long before the dam burst as it neared completion in 1890.

PHOENIX AND TEMPE had begun irrigated farming in the 1880s but were still troubled by floods and drought. In 1902 a federal reclamation program began with the Roosevelt Dam in Salt River Canyon, completed in 1911. Commerce grew also as entrepreneurs such as the Goldwaters and the Babbitts arrived.

Letterhead of the four Babbitt brothers, Arizona's largest mercantile enterprise (Dawn Collection).

The Arizona Graphic

AN
Illustrated Journal
OF
LIFE IN ARIZONA

The *Arizona Graphic* was a large-sized weekly picture magazine published in Phoenix in 1899. This ambitious periodical, produced by Paul Hull, lasted less than a year (picture courtesy William A. Duffen).

PUBLISHING BEGAN in Arizona when a Washington hand press was brought from Ohio in 1859. Though technically obsolete by the 1860s, this press was used to start three news-papers in Arizona. It was obtained originally by William Wrightson, Cincinnati jour-nalist, in 1858 and was carried overland to San Antonio where it was loaded on a wagon train bound for Tubac and the Santa Rita mines. Wrightson, later to lose his life at the hands of the Apache, had assumed the management of the mines. This press printed the first Arizona newspaper, the *Arizonian*, in 1859 (see p. 106) . It was then moved to Tuc-son where J. Howard Wells continued to publish the paper. In April, 1860, a convention at Tucson established a government for the Gadsden Strip and the Mesilla Valley. Wells printed *The Constitution and Schedule of the Provisional Government of Arizona, and the Proceedings of the Convention Held at Tucson.* Although Wells some months be-fore had produced a Spanish imprint (see p. 89) , this may have been the first book print-ed in English.

Here end the Poker Rubaiyat made by Kirke La Shelle. The illustrations were made by F. Holme and hacked out by him with a 3-bladed jackknife on poplar lum-ber carted across-country clear from New York for the purpose. The key-blocks for the initials were made on chalk plates and the whole was made into a book by him at Phoenix, Arizona. Printing was begun De-cember 1, 1902 and finished January 30, 1903. But 274 copies were printed, all on hand-made paper, after which the types were distributed and the plates and color blocks destroyed. 104 copies are for stock-holders of the press and 150 are for sale. This copy is Number 113

A page from *The Poker Rubaiyat* printed at the Bandar Log Press in 1903. John Francis "Frank" Holme operated this private press, the first in the territory, at Phoenix (Courtesy University of Ari-zona Library).

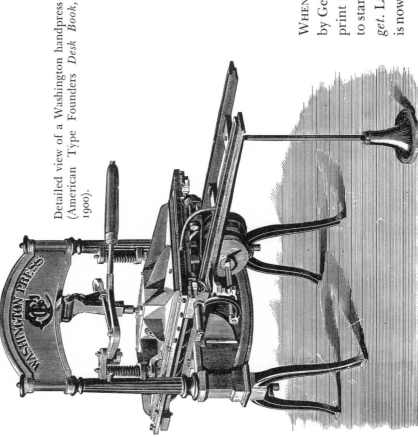

Detailed view of a Washington handpress (American Type Founders *Desk Book*, 1900).

WHEN THE CIVIL WAR came to Arizona, the old Washington press was seized by General Carleton in 1862. After lying dormant a few years it was used to print the *Arizonan* (without the "i") again in 1870-1871 and was then used to start the *Arizona Star*. In 1879 it was taken to Tombstone to print the *Nug-get.* Later it was moved into the office of the Tombstone *Epitaph.* The press is now in the Tubac State Park Museum.

The Tombstone *Epitaph* was one of Arizona's most notable newspapers and was published in the building shown above. John P. Clum launched the paper in 1880; it is still published in the "town too tough to die" (Elliott, 1884).

Another famous Arizona newspaper was the *Arizona Star,* a weekly begun in 1877 by Louis C. Hughes who was governor of the territory, 1893-1896. It is still published at Tucson in conjunction with the *Citizen* (Elliott, 1884).

John Clum, founder of the *Epitaph,* had been Indian agent at the San Carlos reservation, 1874-1877, and then published the *Arizona Citizen* at Florence and Tucson before moving to Tombstone (*Arizona Quarterly,* 1881).

NEWSPAPERS AND SCHOOLS are signs of civilization, and by the eighth decade of the century Arizona had both. Governor Anson P. K. Safford began the public school system in 1871. A month after Safford took office at Tucson, a one-armed veteran of the Civil War with ten men and four boats started down the Colorado River to explore the last unknown part of the United States. It was May 24, 1869, and the explorer was Major John Wesley Powell. Two years later Powell retraced his journey through the Grand Canyon and began the same sort of careful examination that army surveyors had made of most of Arizona in the 1850s. Powell's survey, however, was not intended to open new trails for emigrants; instead it displayed and opened the most incredible natural wonder of the world, the canyon that has become Arizona's trademark and its primary attraction.

Explorer Powell being rescued by G. Y. Bradley from a cliff face near Desolation Canyon, Utah, in 1869. Powell is hanging by his one arm, holding his rescuer's underwear. The artist apparently had the rescuer modestly dress himself before using his underwear as a life rope (Powell, 1895).

Major J. W. Powell. In 1879 he won Congressional approval to establish the Bureau of American Ethnology, and from 1881 to 1894 he headed the U.S. Geological Survey (Winsor, 1889).

THE FIRST MAN through the Grand Canyon may have been James White, a trapper who fled with a companion downstream on a raft to escape Indians in 1867. The companion, Strole, drowned but White made it down to Callville. Powell's party used special boats in 1869 and still had troubles; three men quit and walked off, only to be murdered by Indians.

The Powell party escaping a brush fire that swept their camp on Green River, Colorado, in June, 1869 (Powell, 1895).

Boats of the R. B. Stanton expedition seeking a canyon railroad route in 1889-1890 (*Scribner's*, 1890).

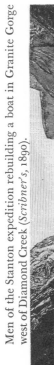

James White losing his companion, George Strole, by drowning in Marble Canyon, 1867 (Bell, 1870).

Men of the Stanton expedition rebuilding a boat in Granite Gorge west of Diamond Creek (*Scribner's*, 1890).

The camp of Lieutenant Ives and Dr. Newberry at the mouth of Diamond Creek in April, 1858. Father Garces probably came this way in 1776, and Powell reached here in 1869. The mountain is Diamond Peak (Möllhausen, 1861).

POWELL MADE IT THROUGH the rapids to the mouth of the Virgin River by the end of August, 1869. Two years later he made a second expedition with a photographer whose work was the basis for over a hundred woodcuts that gave the world its first realistic look at the Canyon. Meantime another surveyor was in the field, Lieutenant George M. Wheeler. In 1871 he took boats up the river from Fort Mohave and reached the mouth of Diamond Creek. Powell's interest in all things scientific led to great and permanent institutions; Wheeler mainly produced maps.

"Big Cañon at the Mouth of Diamond River" by J. J. Young, from a sketch by F. W. Egloffstein (Ives, lithograph on stone, 1861). Compare this with Möllhausen's picture on the opposite page.

The Rio Colorado near the mouth of Diamond Creek, drawn by H. B. Möllhausen. The view is upriver and may be the same rapids shown on an earlier page (Möllhausen, 1861).

The panorama from Point Sublime, drawn by W. H. Holmes for the annual report of the U.S. Geological Survey for 1881. Holmes is considered the greatest topographical artist.

Arizona's most famous robbery: five Gila valley ranchers held up the escort of Paymaster Major J. W. Wham on the Fort Grant-Fort Thomas road in 1889. Painted by Remington from a photograph taken at the scene the day after the robbery (*Harper's Monthly,* 1895).

"A Tombstone Sheriff and Constituents," presumably Johnny Behan; an imaginary picture by an artist who was never in Tombstone (Bishop, 1888).

THE 40,000 WHITE PEOPLE who lived in Arizona by 1878 kept order with relatively few peace officers. As a federal territory, Arizona was assigned one U.S. Marshal who usually rode a desk. All large towns had local marshals, but the principal lawmen were the county sheriffs of whom Bob Paul and John H. Slaughter were good examples. Slaughter was a rancher who came from Texas in the 1870s and settled near Tombstone. After several murders and robberies, plus the gun battle at the O.K. corral in 1881, President Arthur threatened martial law. Although Wyatt Earp fled to Colorado, Sheriff John Behan failed to quell the disorder. In 1887 citizens of Cochise County elected Slaughter, and in a short time he drove out the desperadoes.

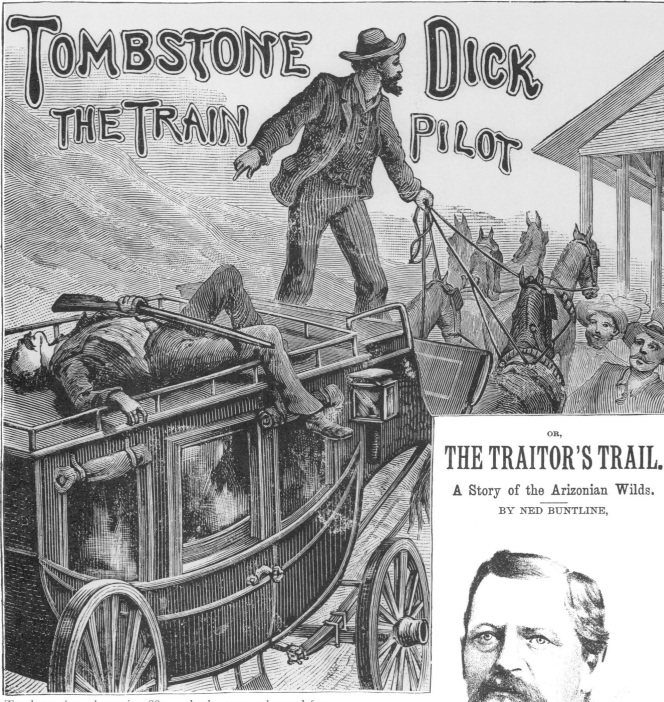

TOMBSTONE DICK
THE TRAIN PILOT

OR,
THE TRAITOR'S TRAIL.
A Story of the Arizonian Wilds.
BY NED BUNTLINE,

Tombstone's outlawry in 1881 made the town a byword for
sin and an inspiration for this dime novel (*Beadle's,* 1885).

Robert H. Paul (Elliott, 1884).

BOB PAUL WAS A Wells Fargo agent who came from California
in 1878. His reputation as a manhunter elevated him to become sheriff of Pima County, serving several terms and never
failing to get his man. He was U.S. Marshal, 1891-93. Another
Arizona law force was the Arizona Rangers who from 1901 to
1909 enforced livestock laws and apprehended felons who
escaped from local authorities.

Gamblers dealing faro; said to be a California scene, but a gambling hall in Prescott or Tucson would have differed little. Roulette and poker were equally popular (*Century*, 1891).

Castle Hot Springs resort, which began in the 1880s as a station on the Phoenix-Wickenburg stage road. The owner furnished towels to passengers who swam in the pools (Higgins, 1911).

Facetiously titled "An Arizona Watering Place," this illustration for an article by a traveling tenderfoot may represent the Agua Caliente ranch near Tucson (Bishop, 1888).

The El Tovar Hotel operated by Fred Harvey on the South Rim of the Grand Canyon. Arizona's most famous resort, it annually draws thousands of tourists from around the world (Higgins, 1911).

John D. Lee was implicated in the 1857 Mountain Meadows Massacre of emigrants in Utah. He escaped prosecution by hiding in Arizona, where he operated a ferry at the mouth of Paria Creek, in 1872. He was executed in 1877 (Clampitt, 1888).

Lee's Ferry on the Colorado south of present Glen Canyon Dam. His crossing continued in use until a bridge was built nearby in 1929 (Beadle, 1881).

A view into the Grand Canyon from the Hance trail. John J. Pershing rode into the canyon from Hance's lodge in 1887 (*Harper's Monthly*, 1890).

John H. Beadle's version of how early tourists could get down into the Canyon (Beadle, 1873).

THE GRAND CANYON was already an international attraction while Arizona was still a territory. The Hopi villages and prehistoric ruins were also known. There were attempts to establish tourist resorts, such as Castle Hot Springs, but Arizona's strange and wonderful sights
were the real magnets. Within the towns, the recreation of the citizens was quite often gambling instead of sightseeing. Every town had its professionals-in-residence, but itinerant sharks
drifted about in numbers until the legislature outlawed gambling in 1907.

Early tourists at the Grand Canyon (*Harper's Monthly*, 1890).

The Powell expedition running a rapid. A down-river trip is still a popular sport using inflated rubber boats, but its hazards still claim lives (Powell, 1875).

AT THE GRAND CANYON, John Hance was the first tourist guide in the 1880s. On the South Rim he hacked out a trail down to Bright Angel Creek. He lodged travelers at his ranch on the rim, and his tall tales became legendary; one guest reported that Hance had dug the Canyon himself as a mining venture! The Santa Fe railway finally ran a branch line from Williams and built the El Tovar Lodge near Hance's Tank in 1902.

The Colorado River at the foot of Bright Angel Trail (Higgins, 1911).

Anson P. K. Safford, third governor (1869-1877), had General Crook assigned to Arizona and brought in the Southern Pacific railway. His mining speculations were a failure (Courtesy Arizona Pioneers' Historical Society).

Governor Richard C. McCormick, journalist and Republican Party organizer in New York, was appointed by Abraham Lincoln as the first territorial secretary. He founded the Prescott *Arizona Miner* and the Tucson *Arizona Citizen* and was a power in politics until 1875 (*Frank Leslie's*, 1863).

Below and continued on opposite page, the constitutional convention in action in December, 1910. Judge Albert C. Baker, standing, helped draft the final version. At Baker's left is E. W. Coker, a Florence lawyer said to have weighed 350 pounds. At the desk is George W. P. Hunt, afterward governor eight times. In the chair, right foreground, is Judge Jacob Weinberger, only member of the 1910 convention still alive (*Arizona Republican*, 1910).

Frederick A. Tritle from Nevada, sixth governor, who presided over the "Thieving Thirteenth" legislature in 1885. It squandered funds but gave Tucson the state university (Elliott, 1884).

"A Flag Day Dream," political cartoon by C. K. Berryman of the Washington *Evening Star*. Berryman originated the Teddy Bear, inspired by Theodore Roosevelt (courtesy Arizona Pioneers' Historical Society).

THERE WERE sixteen federally appointed territorial governors. The first, Goodwin, was elected to Congress in 1864. His successor, McCormick, was an able administrator and Congressional delegate from 1869 to 1875. Governor Safford worked to establish schools and to foster economic development in his long term, 1869-77. The rest were mere political spoilsmen until an Arizona resident, Nathan O. Murphy, was appointed in 1892. Murphy and his successors worked ardently for statehood. Congress finally passed an enabling act in 1910 which led to a constitutional convention. The independent Arizonans became a state on February 14, 1912.

BIBLIOGRAPHY

Appleton's Cyclopaedia of American Biography, 6 vols. New York: D. Appleton, 1889.

Bancroft, Hubert Howe. *History of Arizona and New Mexico, 1530-1888.* San Francisco: History Co., 1889.

Bartlett, John Russell. *Personal Narrative of Explorations and Incidents in Texas, New Mexico, California, Sonora, and Chihuahua . . . ,* 2 vols. New York: D. Appleton, 1854.

Battles and Leaders of the Civil War, 4 vols. New York: The Century Co., 1884-87.

Beadle, John Hanson. *The Undeveloped West.* Philadelphia: National Publ. Co., 1873.

————. *Western Wilds and the Men Who Redeem Them.* Cincinnati: Queen City Book Co., 1881.

Bell, William A. *New Tracks in North America,* 2nd ed. New York: Scribner, Welford, 1870.

Bishop, William Henry. *Mexico, California and Arizona,* new & rev. ed. New York: Harper & Bros., 1888.

Bolton, Herbert E. (ed.). *Anza's California Expeditions,* Vol. III: The San Francisco Colony. Berkeley: Univ. of California Press, 1930.

————. *Font's Complete Diary: A Chronicle of the Founding of San Francisco.* Berkeley: Univ. of California Press, 1933.

Bourke, John G. *The Snake-Dance of the Moquis of Arizona.* London: Sampson Low, Marston, Searle, & Rivington, 1884.

Brandes, Raymond S. *Frontier Military Posts of Arizona.* Globe, Ariz.: Dale Stuart King, 1960. (See below, Government Documents, McDowell.)

Brewerton, George D. *Overland with Kit Carson: A Narrative of the Old Spanish Trail in '48.* New York: Coward-McCann, 1930.

Browne, J. Ross. *Adventures in the Apache Country: A Tour through Arizona and Sonora, with Notes on the Silver Regions of Nevada.* New York: Harper & Bros., 1869.

Campion, J. S. *On the Frontier.* London: Chapman & Hall, 1878.

Clampitt, John W. *Echoes from the Rocky Mountains.* Chicago: National Book Concern, 1888.

Conklin, Enoch. *Picturesque Arizona.* New York: Mining Record, 1878.

Connelley, William Elsey. *War with Mexico, 1846-1847. Doniphan's Expedition and the Conquest of New Mexico and California.* Kansas City, Mo.: Bryant & Douglas, 1907.

Cozzens, Samuel Woodworth. *The Marvellous Country.* Boston: Shepard & Gill, 1873.

Davis, W. W. H. *El Gringo, or New Mexico and Her People.* New York: Harper & Bros., 1857.

Dellenbaugh, Frederick S. *The Romance of the Colorado River.* New York: G. P. Putnam's Sons, 1904.

DeQuille, Dan (William Wright). *History of the Big Bonanza.* San Francisco: A. L. Bancroft, 1877.

Desk Book of Type Specimens. New York: American Type Founders Co., 1900.

Dunn, Jacob Piatt. *Massacres of the Mountains: A History of the Indian Wars of the Far West.* New York: Harper & Bros., 1886.

Elliott, Wallace W. & Co. *History of Arizona Territory Showing Its Resources and Advantages.* San Francisco: 1884.

Engelhardt, Zephyrin. *The Franciscan in Arizona.* Harbor Springs, Mich.: Holy Childhood Indian School, 1899.

Flint, Timothy (ed.). *The Personal Narrative of James O. Pattie of Kentucky.* Cincinnati: John H .Wood, 1831.

Fröbel, Julius. *Aus Amerika: Erfahrungen, Reisen und Studien,* 2 vols. Leipzig: Verlagsbuchhandlung von J. J. Weber, 1857.

Frost, John. *Thrilling Adventures Among the Indians.* Philadelphia: J. W. Bradley, 1850.

Gleed, Charles S. (ed.). *Guide from the Missouri River to the Pacific Ocean via Kansas, Colorado, New Mexico, Arizona, and California* (title varies). Chicago: Rand, McNally, 1882.

————. *Idem,* 1885.

Gray, Andrew Belcher. *Survey of a Route for the Southern Pacific R. R., on the 32nd Parallel, . . . for the Texas Western R. R. Company.* Cincinnati: Railroad Record, 1856.

Hamilton, Patrick. *The Resources of Arizona,* Third Edition. San Francisco: A. L. Bancroft, 1884.

Higgins, Charles A. *New Guide to the Pacific Coast, Santa Fe Route.* Chicago: Rand, McNally, 1895.

————. *To California over the Santa Fe Trail.* Chicago: Santa Fe R.R., 1911.

Hinton, Richard J. *The Hand-Book to Arizona: Its Resources, History, Towns, Mines, Ruins and Scenery.* San Francisco: Payot, Upham, 1878.

Ingham, G. Thomas. *Digging Gold Among the Rockies.* Philadelphia: Hubbard Bros., 1880.

James, George Wharton. *The Wonders of the Colorado Desert,* 2 vols. Boston: Little, Brown, 1906.

————. *Indian Blankets and Their Makers.* Chicago: A. C. McClurg, 1914.

Kelsey, D. M. *History of Our Wild West and Stories of Pioneer Life.* Chicago: Thompson & Thomas, 1901.

Kent, Henry Brainard. *Graphic Sketches of the West.* Chicago: R. R. Donnelley & Sons, 1890.

La Shelle, Kirke. *The Poker Rubaiyat.* Phoenix: Bandar Log Press, 1902.

Lossing, Benson J. *Pictorial Field Book of the Civil War in America.* Hartford: 1876-78.

Loza, Don Pedro. *Carta Pastoral del Obispo de Sonora.* Tucson: Weekly Arizonian, 1859.

Lummis, Charles F. *Some Strange Corners of Our Country.* New York: The Century Co., 1892.

Mansfield, Edward D. *The Mexican War.* New York: A. S. Barnes, 1848.

Miles, Nelson A. *Personal Recollections and Observations of General Nelson A. Miles . . .* Chicago: The Werner Co., 1896.

Moat, Louis Shepheard (ed.). *Frank Leslie's Illustrated Famous Leaders and Battle Scenes of the Civil War.* New York: Mrs. Frank Leslie, 1896.

Möllhausen, Balduin. *Reisen in die Felsengebirge Nord-Amerikas bis zum Hoch-Plateau von Neu-Mexico,* 2 vols. Leipzig: Hermann Costenoble, 1861.

Mowry, Sylvester. *Memoir of the Proposed Territory of Arizona.* Washington: Henry Polkinhorn, 1857.

Navajo Bible. Chicago: American Bible Society, 1918.

Olmstead, R. R. (ed.). *Scenes of Wonder and Curiosity from Hutchings' California Magazine, 1856-1861.* Berkeley: Howell-North, 1962.

Poston, Charles D. *Apache-Land.* San Francisco: A. L. Bancroft, 1878.

Powell, J. W. *Canyons of the Colorado.* Meadville, Pa.: Flood & Vincent, 1895.

Prose and Poetry of the Live Stock Industry of the United States. Denver: National Live Stock Assn., 1905.

Pumpelly, Raphael. *Across America and Asia.* New York: Leypoldt & Holt, 1870.

Ringwalt, J. Luther (ed.). *American Encyclopedia of Printing.* Philadelphia: Menamin & Ringwalt, 1871.

Roberts, Edward. *With the Invader: Glimpses of the Southwest.* San Francisco: Samuel Carson, 1885.

Shearer, Frederick E. (ed.). *The Pacific Tourist.* New York: Adams & Bishop, 1884.

Sidney, Margaret. *The Golden West, As Seen by the Ridgway Club.* Boston: D. Lothrop Co., 1886.

Steele, James W. *Rand McNally & Company's New Overland Guide to the Pacific Coast.* Chicago: Rand, McNally, 1890.

Stratton, R. B. *Captivity of the Oatman Girls,* 3rd ed. New York: Carleton & Porter, 1858.

Sweetser, M. F. *King's Handbook of the United States.* Buffalo, N.Y.: Moses King Corp., 1892.

Thayer, William M. *Marvels of the New West.* Norwich, Conn.: Henry Bill Publ. Co., 1888.

Twitchell, Ralph E. *The Leading Facts of New Mexican History,* 2 vols. Cedar Rapids, Iowa: Torch Press, 1912.

Ullastre, Evaristo (ed.). *Museo Militar: Historia, Indumentaria, Armas, Sistemas de Combate, Instituciones, Organización del Ejercito Español,* 3 vols. Barcelona: 1884.

Winsor, Justin. *Narrative and Critical History of America,* 8 vols. Boston: Houghton, Mifflin, 1889.

Wonderful Adventures: A Series of Narratives of Personal Experiences among the Native Tribes of America, 2nd ed. Philadelphia: J. B. Lippincott, 1874.

Wood, Stanley. *Over the Range to the Golden Gate.* Chicago: R. R. Donnelley, 1903.

NEWSPAPERS AND PERIODICALS

The Arizona Graphic, 1899.
Arizona Live Stock Journal, 1884.
Arizona Quarterly Illustrated, 1881.
Arizona Republican, 1910.
Beadle's Dime Library, 1885.
Beadle's Half Dime Library, 1887.
The Century Illustrated Monthly Magazine, 1882-1902.
Daily Graphic, 1878.
Engineering and Mining Journal, 1881.
Harper's New Monthly Magazine, 1878-1898.
Hutchings' California Magazine, 1856-1861. (See above, Olmstead.)
Frank Leslie's Illustrated News, 1863, 1883.
Land of Sunshine, 1900.
Outing, 1886-1888.
Scribner's Magazine, 1890.
Tombstone Epitaph, 1886.
Weekly Arizonian, 1859.

GOVERNMENT DOCUMENTS

Emory, William H. *Notes of a Military Reconnoissance from Fort Leavenworth, in Missouri, to San Diego, in California, Including Parts of the Arkansas, Del Norte, and Gila Rivers.* Senate Exec. Doc. 7, 30th Cong., 1st sess. Washington: 1848.

Ives, Joseph C. *Report upon the Colorado River of the West, Explored in 1857 and 1858 . . .* Senate Exec. Doc., 36th Cong., 1st sess. Washington: 1861.

McDowell, Major General Irvin. *Outline Descriptions of Pacific Military Posts in the Military Division of the Pacific.* San Francisco: 1877.

Parke, John G. *Report of Explorations for Railroad Routes . . . near the 32d Parallel of North Latitude . . . 1854-5.* Vol. 7 of House Exec. Doc. 91, 33rd Cong., 2nd sess. Washington: 1857.

Powell, John Wesley. *Exploration of the Colorado River of the West and Its Tributaries.* Washington: 1875.

Simpson, James H. *The Report of Lieutenant J. H. Simpson of an Expedition into the Navajo Country in 1849.* Senate Exec. Doc. 64, 31st Cong., 1st sess. Washington: 1850.

Sitgreaves, Lorenzo. *Report of an Expedition down the Zuni and Colorado Rivers.* Senate Exec. Doc., 33rd Cong., 1st sess. Washington: 1854.

U.S. Department of Agriculture, Bureau of Animal Husbandry. *Special Report on the History and Present Condition of the Sheep Industry of the United States.* House Misc. Doc. 105, 52nd Cong., 2nd sess. Washington: 1892.

U.S. Bureau of American Ethnology. *Annual Report,* 1880-81, 1881-82, 1906-07. Washington: 1881, 1882, 1907.

U.S. Department of the Interior, National Park Service. *Historic American Buildings Survey.* Washington: 1941.

U.S. Bureau of the Census. *Report on Indians Taxed and Not Taxed of the United States at the Eleventh Census.* Washington: 1890.

Whipple, Amiel Weeks. *Report of Explorations for a Railway Route, near the Thirty-Fifth Parallel of North Latitude . . . 1853-4.* Washington: 1856.

SPECIAL COLLECTIONS

Arizona State Library and Archives, Phoenix.

Dawn Collection, Ariz. Pioneers' Historical Society Library, Tucson.

Duffen, William A., private collection, Tucson.

Jenson Collection, Ariz. Pioneers' Historical Society, Tucson.

Serven, James E., library of, Tucson.

INDEX

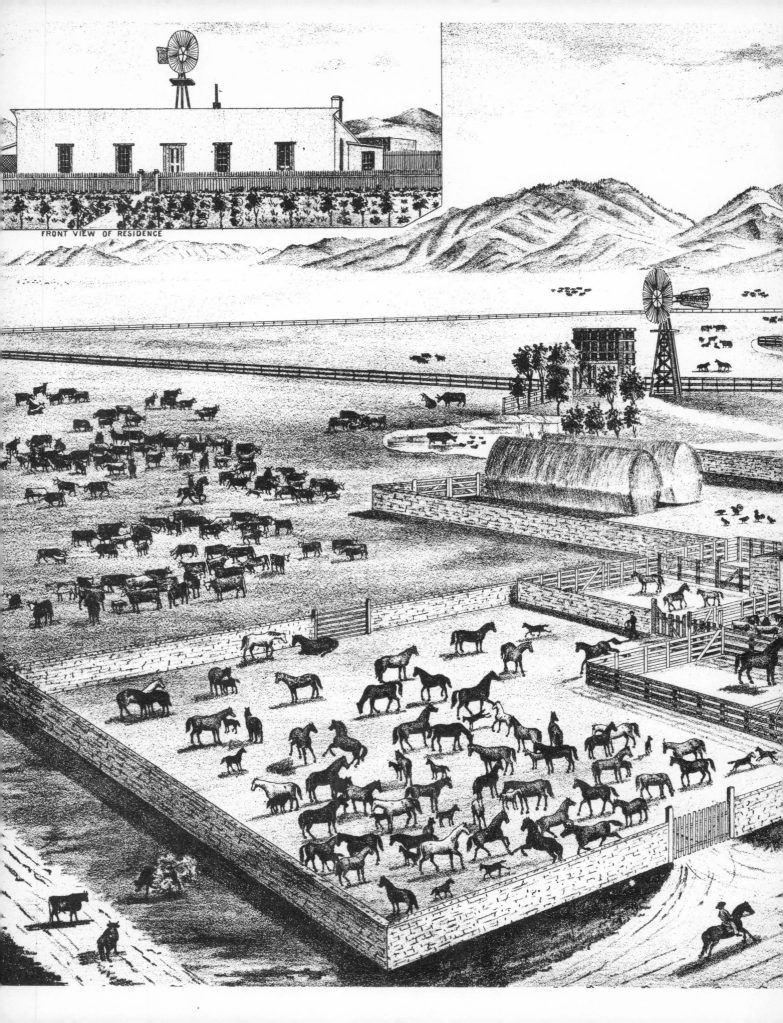

FRONT VIEW OF RESIDENCE